Hooves High

and other tails from across the cube wall

Paul Mitchell and Nicole White

ISBN: 1496163923
ISBN 13: 9781496163929

This is dedicated to all our fellow hoofers.

Give in to your funny bone and that tickle in your heart. It's what promotes community, laughter, and positivity, and more importantly, builds strong relationships. And remember… keep making sweet-ass lemonade with those lemons, no matter how sour they are.

Hooves High!

Contents

Acknowledgments

Paul and Nicole Would Like to Thank:

Our patient and very talented illustrator, Thom Phelps. Thank you for enduring our constant changes and questions. HH Pig, and his hooves, look great!

Our photographer, Jesse Scimeca, at Made Legit Media, for making us look good. Don't forget the little people when you become famous. We want to come to your first "real" red-carpet premiere!

Our awesome editor, Dana Campbell. You got us; you really got us! Thank you for your careful review, encouragement, and suggestions. We sincerely appreciate it. Until next time!

Our work families over the years, especially our CSI teammates. Thank you for making those long work days (and some nights) so much fun. You've made us better people, peers, managers, and leaders.

Our first hoofer, Marie, and our third musketeer, Queen Tina. Your hoof prints are forever on our hearts.

Paul Would Additionally Like To Thank:

My wife, Marilyn, for allowing me the freedom and time to write this and for supporting me every step of the way. Also, thank you for letting me eat as much cookie dough as I want with no judgment. I love you!

My children, Brennan, Ryan, and Megan, and my other children, Ali, Rian, and Theo, for being a constant source of entertainment (and stories)! You are each special and unique, and you have brought so much joy and fulfillment to my life. I love you. Also, thank you, Theo, for being my sometimes editor and ensuring I always know just how *old* I really am.

My parents, Paul and Nancy, who have always encouraged and supported me in whatever I want to do. Thank you for being my never-ending rocks. Love, Newt.

Finally, Nicole, my BFF, partner-in-crime, and dessert-sharer. You are such a fun and uplifting presence, and I can't tell you how truly lucky I feel to have found you. My hooves stretch high in the air and do the happy dance every time we're together, and I have loved every minute of this experience with you. Thank you (and my cookies are not salty!). Hooves High!

Nicole would Additionally Like to Thank:

First and foremost, I want to acknowledge God who guides me through this labyrinth of life, even when I don't always listen, and loves me unconditionally. I am his perfect creation.

My beautiful children, Kenneth, Autumn, and Gabriele, for making me the youthful person I am. It's because of you that my outlook on life is so positive and hopeful. I believe in all that you are and love you immensely.

My mom, Susan, for being the woman and mother you are. It was because of you that I am the confident, sassy, sexy, vibrant woman that I am. Ich liebe dich, mutti! (*I love you, mom!*)

Last, but definitely not least, Paul. You'll never know just how much your (and Mar's) friendship has meant to me over these years. I looked forward to coming to work every day for all the fun, and the crazy, that we had. Thank you, my friend, for sharing

Mitchell-Land with me, for helping me stay sane and positive when I wanted to let my not-so-nice twin out, and for helping to make a dream come true. Can't wait to sit next to you on Ellen's couch. Hooves High!

Introduction

Dear Reader,

We're so happy you've picked up a copy of our book! With all the stress we experience in our everyday lives, whether it is at home or in the office, wouldn't it be great if you could just laugh it all away? Well, sit back, grab a piece of key-lime cheesecake (well, that's what we would eat), and be prepared to become a laugh whore!

We met each other at work several years ago. Total opposites in many ways, Nicole, a sassy, sexy mulatta, and Paul, a towering, corn-fed 'Bama Boy, realized we had a couple of big things in common. We both promote building strong relationships personally and professionally and, just as importantly, we both live *out loud!* In other words, we talk to anyone (including the brick walls), constantly meet hilarious people (whether they know it or not), find ourselves in the funniest situations (like Nicole's "Santa's Thong" incident), laugh at the most inappropriate times (cue our "Mondo!" distress call), and come up with some of the craziest catch phrases to commemorate those moments (Embrace Your Bigness - EYB). Since then, we've found something almost every day that either makes Nicole's mascara run or Paul's sides hurt (only because Paul doesn't wear mascara) from laughing so hard.

This book will make you laugh your ass off and hopefully learn to laugh at yourself. Each chapter provides a catch phrase and the hilarious personal story (or two) that helped shape its meaning for us. The chapters contain four parts:

1. The Meaning (definition of the catch phrase)
2. The Heart of the Story (when to use it—because you *will* want to use it!)
3. The Tail (how it came about)
4. Trimming the Fat (the lesson learned).

Finally, we share our secret weapon for success: food! You'll love our potluck recipes for victory because nothing gets you through the day like a good scoop of Shiznit Spinach Dip or Cat Barf.

You can bring your new positive and hilarious attitude back to the cube farm at work and infiltrate others with it. Also, we want you to learn to enjoy food again (without the guilt – EYB!) and incorporate this love into the office as well.

In other words, we want your workplace to be your happy place! So, open up and say "ahh" because you're about to get fed a heaping helping of our off-brand humor, complete with catch phrases, the hot-flash inducing "tails" that accompany them, the life lessons we learned as a result, and a side of our no-fail favorite foods to help feed your stomach, as well as your soul, along the way.

Hooves High!
Paul & Nicole

Hooves High

Meaning

If you're the one on your team always suggesting a potluck, then your hooves are high! In other words, you love food.

Heart of the Story

If you're looking to get healthy in the workplace, *this is not your book*. We're not going to be spouting off weight loss tips and nutritional goals, so hear us when we tell you *we love food*. We are not the type of people who can eat and eat and not gain a pound. If that's you, and you're reading this book, we hate you. (In fact, we both gained five pounds just by writing down these recipes.) Your hooves can still be high but, if we ever meet you, be prepared for snide remarks and occasional snubs. What we'd really like to do is kick your skinny ass, but since you love food, we'll accept you as the stepbrother or stepsister that's the necessary evil. We just suggest you say little and agree always.

[NICOLE'S NOTE: *And bow. We like bowing.*]

We are the type of people, though, who love chicken biscuits in the morning with a side of heffa juice (aka gravy for you non-southerners) and coffee from the gas station down the street with three full squirts of French vanilla concentrated creamer that contains all the original fat from the French vanilla cow. We're also the type of people who decide where to go for lunch based on the restaurant's dessert menu (i.e. key lime cheesecake!). We coordinate events at work that involve food, and we make friends with other departments who like to host food-related functions as well.

Something else you need to know before we continue is, if Paul had a mistress, her name would be Chocolate Surprise (and, no we don't mean Beyoncé, his favorite singer).

[PAUL'S NOTE: *Yes, it would; yes, it is; and I'll share the recipe with you later in the book.*]

Undeniably, Paul is a dessert whore. A fantasy three-course meal to him consists of an appetizer of cookies, followed by an entrée of cake, and rounded out with a nice dessert of something a la mode! We thought Paul would waste away into nothing when whipped cream frosting became all the rage a few years ago and he (the true Hoofer he is) started refusing cake (bless his heart). Thank goodness for all the doctors who've come out recently proclaiming the truth about real butter versus that margarine spread containing "mono" something or other that you can't even pronounce unless you start at the end and work your way backward (kinda like reading a German word). Yes, butter cream frosting is back, and we're so glad Paul is whole again.

[PAUL'S NOTE: *Indeed!* Eight pounds, six ounces!]

 *Tail*

There are some moments in life where you just go, "Shit, they got me," and you're left with only two choices:

1. You can either continue to lie and hope the other person's bullshit radar is on the fritz.
2. You can face the truth head on, as ugly as it may be, and fess up to the crime. One such incident happened to Paul a few years back.

Soon after Paul and Nicole met at work, they discovered they each had a love affair with food--Paul with desserts and Nicole with everything else.

[NICOLE'S NOTE: *Wait! Why do I have to be the one labeled as liking "everything else"? That makes me sound like a cow!*]
[PAUL'S NOTE: *Well, if the moo fits...*]

One of their first work-related challenges was to figure out how to bring several teams of disparate individuals together to work more cohesively and collectively. The standard manager tricks of holding team meetings and giving presentations weren't going to work, so Paul and Nicole planned a potluck instead. It was perfect because food is the universal language, and they knew it would give everyone some common ground to start conversations.

[PAUL'S NOTE: *And it satisfied Nicole's insatiable need for food. Moooo!*]
[NICOLE'S NOTE: *I hope Baby Jesus comes down from heaven and drop-kicks yo ass for saying that!*]
[PAUL'S NOTE: *There is no drop-kickin' when the truth's being told. Hallelujah!*]
[NICOLE'S NOTE: *My ass! Let's just amend the initial comment. "It satisfied our insatiable need"...cause Lord knows I didn't pack on all this weight until I began lunchin' with you!*]
[PAUL'S NOTE: *Mmnt.*]

Nicole, always on the ready for a good potluck, whipped out her handy-dandy Perfect Potluck Matrix and went to work. She put together sign-up sheets and coordinated the entrees, veggies, starches and desserts needed, based on the number of people attending.

[NICOLE'S NOTE: *And I'll show you how to plan the perfect potluck for your own team or family gathering a little later!*]

If someone started to waiver on whether or not they would participate, Nicole turned up the guilt and made them feel as useless as a back pocket on a shirt.

[NICOLE'S NOTE: *Because guilt is the gift that keeps on giving <wink>.*]

She would say in her best Becky voice, "Oh, you're not coming? Why not? I was so looking forward to talking to you, and now I'll be stuck with *<insert name of their nemesis>*. Well, hell. And you know how much everyone enjoys your *<insert food>*. I hope no one else bails 'cause you know the rest of the team kind of follows your lead. Are you sure you can't come?"

Ninety-nine point nine percent of the time, whomever Nicole was talking to either felt so guilty or so flattered they'd not only show up, but they'd make something extra complicated and delicious.

[PAUL'S NOTE: *For those of you who are white, like me, "Becky" is Ebonics for white girl. There's even a song about it. Look it up.*]

Paul and Nicole always wrangled at least twenty people to participate in a potluck at any given time, and there was always so much food you could feed a fat camp full of starving kids and even have some left over to end a little bit of world hunger. At one particular potluck, food covered the appetizer table, an entrée table and, most important, a big fat dessert table. Once Nicole gave the okay to start digging in, Paul quickly make his way through the line with a small plate of appetizers and entrées. Then, as if the table would magically disappear once he sat down, Paul bee-lined for the desserts, neatly piling one of each on his plate.

"What the hell?" Nicole exclaimed loudly for all to hear.

"What?" Paul shot back, unapologetically.

"Look at all that damn dessert!"

"I got a plate of real food first. What do you want from me? These nice people took the time to make all these desserts, and I feel obligated to try each one."

And, with that, Paul sat down without another word, picked through his entrée plate, ensuring he did not fill up on meat and vegetables, and worked his way through his mountainous dessert plate.

About ten minutes later, Paul tried to casually make his way back over to the dessert table for round two, in a move affectionately Nicole dubbed as *The Sneak*. Paul would stop and speak to a person here and a person there, giving the illusion he was "working the room", when all he was really doing was inching his way back to his mistress.

Instantly recognizing The Sneak, Nicole called Paul out. "Don't think I don't know where you're going!"

"What?" Paul said, again in the most unapologetic of tones.

"You're getting a second plate of dessert!" The belittlement cut through the air like a knife.

With tilted head and raised brow, Paul simply replied, "And? Your point?"

"Well, aren't we just a little piggy today! Oink! Oink!" she imitated, with her eyes pinched and her nose crinkled in true pig-like fashion.

[PAUL'S NOTE: *Nicole swears she did not make pig noises, but it was all so hurtful and traumatic that's it's hard to remember for sure now.*]

[NICOLE'S NOTE: *Traumatic?! Who's being the drama queen now?*]
[PAUL'S NOTE: *It cut...deep!*]
[NICOLE'S NOTE: *DQ, man...DQ!*]

In a hopeless situation, with everyone looking up at him and his empty plate perched menacingly over the red velvet cake, Paul simply replied, "Excuse me?"

[PAUL'S NOTE: *So, this was the moment. The moment when you know you're caught, and I was caught real good, with my fork in mid-stab over that cake. My first instinct was to deny, deny, deny but, as you'll soon see, I finally just gave up and faced the music.*]

By now, people had caught the scent of the "goings down" in the air, and the buzz of their many conversations became conspicuously quiet. After all, they knew when Nicole and Paul started going at it; something unexpected was bound to happen.

Realizing he had to deflect and beat Nicole to her next punch line, Paul frantically stated, "I don't care. If I'm a pig, so be it. My hooves are high!"

He reached down, stabbed the red velvet cake right off the platter, and shoveled a huge piece into his snout. With red-stained teeth and icing clinging to his chin, Paul smiled at Nicole as if saying, "What you gonna say now?" The *bitch* was implied.

What ensued next can only be described as sheer mayhem. Appetizers were choked on, soda shot out of noses. People were laughing so hard. They tried to clean up the messes, but all eyes remained fixed on Paul. In a final moment of defiance, Paul threw his arms up, spread his middle fingers apart, and exclaimed for all to hear, "*Hooves High!*"

With trepidation, Paul saw a couple of people quietly spread their fingers apart, trying to imitate the movement. He encouraged, "If you love food and are tired of being polite and only taking a small portion here or there, hold your hands high. Screw convention! Hi, my name is Paul, and I am a dessert whore! Hooves High!"

With his hands still high, he scanned the crowd for support. Seconds ticked by like hours. Paul's eyes darted back and forth as he hoped for vindication. Finally, a voice from the back called, "My name is Marie, and I love wings! All kinds, and my Hooves are High, too!" A chicken wing was grasped proudly in her hoof as proof, and she started laughing.

[PAUL'S NOTE: *Marie was already one of my favorite people, but she will forever be cemented in my heart as the first official hoofer in our Hooves High Club. Love you, Marie!*]

Quickly, others confessed to their food affairs, too. It was great. There were no apologies. Just acceptance. And so, a new mantra emerged. From a situation meant to disparage and cause dejection, empowerment was born. Hooves High was embraced as a powerful catch phrase used by all--from the skinny analyst on our team who looked like a zipper when she stuck out her tongue to the managers who insisted they be referred to as tall and not tubby. Yes, Hooves High gave you permission to love your food in the open instead of hiding it behind a cheater's closed door.

[PAUL & NICOLE'S NOTE: *We do want to extend our apologies to the pig. Unfortunately, that poor little pink animal has been maligned for centuries as being synonymous with overeating and obesity, so who are we to try and change that now? We're just going to embrace it by keeping our snouts clean and our Hooves High.*]

Nicole now regrets her malicious behavior toward Paul and firmly believes fellow hoofers should never call each other out. The best way to support a fellow hoofer is to either join in or simply turn a blind eye and provide a nonjudgmental antacid when needed.

Setting Free your Inner Hoof

So, when can you release your inner hoof? Below are some appropriate situations when a full-on Hooves High exclamation is fitting:

1. The next time you're in a team meeting and someone produces a birthday cake to celebrate a coworker's birthday. Hooves High!
2. When the project manager of a project you've been slaving over brings in doughnuts from your favorite doughnut place and they're the good kind, topped with icing or filled with fruit fillings. Hooves High!
3. When a vendor pops in with fresh bagels, a variety of flavored cream cheeses, and the good coffee during a presentation to try and sell you on the latest product. Hooves High!
4. If management asks you to go to lunch with them and they tell you they're buying…before you order. Hooves High!

[PAUL & NICOLE'S NOTE: *We fully support loud bursts of Hooves High; however, unless you have already trained your boss in your quirky behaviors, it's usually better to keep your outbursts to a minimum in one-on-one situations, as you run the risk of your boss thinking you need psychiatric attention. At these moments, Hooves High at your own risk!*]

The Hooves High Hand Gesture

Raise your arms high in the air and make the Vulcan "Live Long and Prosper" sign with both hands, then bring your thumbs back across your palms to imitate two hooves, and repeat after us: *Hooves High!*

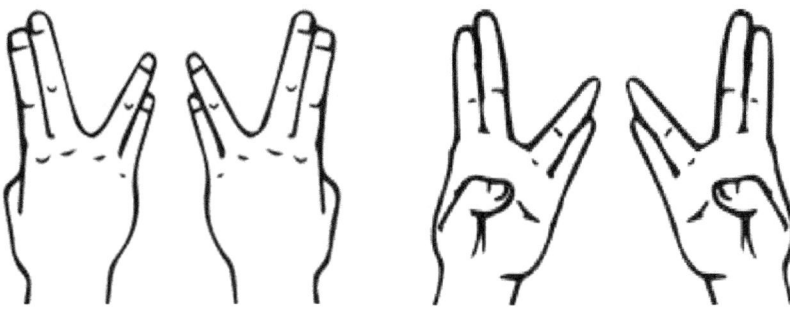

Trimming the Fat

Don't pass judgment on others (especially when food is involved). We all have our quirks and, if you're reading this book, yours probably include food, fun, laughter and more fun. Remember, we each live in a glass house and, just as quickly as you can pass judgment, judgment can be passed on you (like a bad kidney stone), especially in the workplace. Stay open, and know that remaining as nonjudgmental as possible will take you the farthest.

Mmnt!

Meaning

"Mmnt!" is an expression of displeasure. It's easy and simple to say, and it sounds better than "You stupid bitch" or "Damn, now I'm gonna have to work all night because your dumb ass just screwed up!"

Heart of the Story

The correct pronunciation of "Mmnt!" is very important because it's really more of a sound than a word. The *t* is almost silent. Lord knows you don't ever want to be caught mispronouncing a word at work and appearing unprofessional (even a made-up one like this). So, repeat after us: it's MMNt and not mmnT.

The amount of emphasis and the loudness of your voice should be equal to the amount of aggravation or anger you're experiencing. For instance, if you come into work and forget your ID badge, a small "Mmnt!" will probably do. It really can only be heard by you and typically will not produce a response from other people who may have heard you and understand what the word means.

Let's say, though, you are running late for work, have a big presentation to give in five minutes, and you realize after you get to the door that you left your ID badge and your notes for the meeting at home. In that case, a big, loud "Mmnt!" for all to hear is totally appropriate and justified. With that kind of frustration, coworkers should come flocking to your side, asking what they can do to help. If they don't, they're not your friends, and you can write them off your Christmas list.

"Mmnt!" isn't just an expression of frustration for your own actions. It is a very fitting comment about others' actions as well. When end users still call you for help even after you've trained them, provided dummy-proof documentation and explained the same thing three times, throw a well-deserved "Mmnt!" their way. When someone trips, *again*, on the hall carpet square that's needed replacing for months and it's in front of an audience, look them dead in the eye and go, "Mmnt!" Frankly, they should have known.

Finally, "Mmnt!" is a great phrase you can use in your everyday life. When your husband says he can't do something because football season has started, and it dawns on you that for the next few Saturdays and Sundays his ass is going to be parked on the couch in front of the TV: "Mmnt!" Or when your wife drops the bomb that you'll be going to Sunday dinner at her mother's house at 4:00 p.m. (aka the start time for game two) when she lives an hour away (meaning you'll miss how game one ends and you won't get home until after game three begins), a low-toned "Mmnt!" is appropriate. Or when the kids have ignored you for the third time, a forceful "MMNT!" is all you'll need to let them know they are seconds away from being knocked into next week.

[NICOLE'S NOTE: *Guys, when it comes to your wife or girlfriend, always use a low-toned "Mmnt!" We don't want to hear on the news about how you ended up in the hospital with gunshot wounds.*]

Tail

"Mmnt!" is so versatile that we couldn't pick just one tail to share with you, so we selected three. They will illustrate the adaptability and flexibility one simple four-letter word can have. Unlike those other four-letter words we all know and love, this is a new one that's appropriate no matter what kind of company you're keeping.

1. SALTY COOKIES

As we mentioned, potlucks are Paul and Nicole's specialty. At the end of one potluck, they immediately begin planning the next one because, well, why not? Not only are they great opportunities for Hoofers to try lots of different foods but, most importantly, they're an opportunity to have others cook. Let's face it, who doesn't love that?

At the end of their first year together, it was time for the big Christmas/Hanukkah/Kwanzaa potluck and Nicole was all atwitter, signing up peeps for different dishes and desserts. All year, Paul had bragged and bragged about his "famous" Merry Christmas cookies. He claimed to have adoring fans far and wide that put in special requests for his cookies during the holidays. Knowing Paul would be debuting his cookies for her and the team at this potluck, Nicole quickly assigned him one of the coveted dessert spots.

As the potluck approached, Paul walked by Nicole's office and called out, "Only two more days til I bless you with my Merry Christmas cookies."

Nicole, eager to lay her greedy hands on this wondrously hyped cookie, yelled back, "Ooh, sweetie, you know I can't wait. Mama loves her a cookie! You make sure I get the first one!"

For the next two days, Paul continued to build the frenzy over his heavenly baked treats. On the day of the potluck, Paul purposely arrived five minutes late so he could make a grand entrance. After surveying the best door for his entrance (because there were two), he flung open the door farthest from the food and proudly marched in carrying a large red plate full of shortbread cookies topped with rich, buttery icing. As he moved through the crowd, he gave everyone the head nod indicating that, yes, they were indeed among greatness.

With a sweep of his hand, Paul quickly pushed aside all inferior desserts on the dessert table to make room for his Merry Christmas cookies in the center. No one seemed to mind, as it was understood that these cookies deserved a place of prominence and distinction.

After everyone enjoyed a round or two of appetizers, starches, entrées and vegetables, it was time for dessert. Paul swiftly made his way to the back of the room to hand out his cookies so as to divert attacks from any wayward cookie vultures.

[PAUL'S NOTE: *You know who you are.*]

He gently placed one cookie on each person's plate and sat down, waiting for the oohs, ahhs and other accolades to begin. Nicole was the first to speak. Paul turned to her in anticipation.

"What the fuck is this?"

"I know," Paul beamed, understanding Nicole was *verklempt* and forgiving her use of the f-bomb in front of the team. "Fabulous, aren't they?" he enthused.

"Fabulously salty, I'd say. Did you screw up the recipe?" Nicole shot back.

"What?" Paul exclaimed, with a look of horror on his face. "Let me taste one." Jumping up, he ran to the back of the room and shoved a cookie in his mouth. "No, these are perfect, as always. I don't know what you're talking about. They're not salty!"

"Oh yes, they are," she insisted. "I need a glass of water." <cough> <cough>

"You need to stop fronting and admit they're the best cookie you've ever had," Paul replied, only half kidding now.

"No, I'm serious. These are the saltiest cookies I've ever tasted."

"What? Are you kidding me? You are obviously sick, and your taste buds are distorted." Paul frowned in displeasure.

Paul scanned the room and saw others looking down at their cookies, debating whether or not to taste them, so he continued,

"Look, everyone, you need to try them. Don't let the Hater-Ade Nicole is drinking sway you. My cookies are *not* salty!"

With that, a few people bit into their cookies, and several oohs and ahhs floated around. Hearing them, Paul immediately picked up his pride off the floor and began to dust it off. Simultaneously, he shot Nicole his best skunk eye with a hint of "told you so, bitch."

"Eww, these really are kinda salty," came a hateful minion from the front of the room.

Bam! Paul's pride fell back onto the dirty, carpeted floor. "Really?" he said. "Are you sure it's not just Nicole using her powers of suggestive thinking on you?"

"No, they are salty. I'm sorry."

"Yeah, I can see where you'd say they're salty," said another spiteful underling. "I'm not complaining, because the cookie is great, but I do taste the salt in them."

"Honestly, there is *no* salt in these cookies, people! No one has ever said this before!" Paul moaned. "I am in a state of shock."

"Well, it looks like about seventy percent of the peeps like them, so maybe only those of us with a more refined palate were able to pick up on all the saltiness," Nicole offered, clearly pleased with herself.

Paul stared at her. "Seventy percent, my ass. You have poisoned everyone's mind with your salt talk. If you'd have never said it, no one else would have said anything," Paul responded bitterly. "But perhaps you're right about being a salt connoisseur." <wink, wink>

"You did not just go there, Mr. Mitchell!" Nicole gasped in mock disgust. "I will have HR down here faster than Monica turned on Bill with that blue dress! And you know black girls, even the mulatta ones like myself, don't do that. It's a white girl thing! Mmnt!" And there it is, the *Mmnt*.

"Okay, okay," Paul said laughing and throwing his hands up in defeat. "I guess I'll just have to accept seventy percent for now, but this debate is far from over."

"Yes, perhaps by this time next year you'll have had enough time to figure out how to make the next batch less salty."

[NICOLE'S NOTE: *And every year since then, someone has commented on their saltiness.*]
[PAUL'S NOTE: *Yes, because every year you bring it up before they are able to form their own opinions! Mmnt!*] And there it is again.
[NICOLE'S NOTE: *I'm just trying to prepare them for the shock.*]
[PAUL'S NOTE: *Yeah, go on. Take another sip of your Hater-Ade.*]

2. RED CROSS RETRIBUTION

Let's share another example of when "Mmnt!" is appropriate. Paul and Nicole regularly donate blood to the Red Cross. They both have type O blood and feel it's important to give as often as possible.

[PAUL'S NOTE: *I have an O negative blood type, so that makes me the universal donor and slightly more important than Nicole, who only has O positive.*]
[NICOLE'S NOTE: *"Only" my ass! O positive is still important, and it's even better because I can receive blood from both O positive and O negative donors! You can only receive blood from other O negatives!*]
[PAUL'S NOTE: *Don't go bitch cakes on me. I'm just saying it's not the best…like mine.*]
[NICOLE'S NOTE: *Mmnt! At least I won't die a lonely death waiting for blood!*]

Because Paul spent some time out of the country recently, he was on a "deferred" status for a year and unable to give blood. Some of his favorite things about giving blood, though, are the peanut butter cookies and juice they offer after every donation. He was often spotted pumping his fist in increasing frenzy while donating just to get his peanut butter cookies faster.

[PAUL'S NOTE: *Hooves High!*]

One time, during Paul's deferment period, Nicole came back from giving blood in a particularly good mood. After extolling the virtues and importance of giving blood and making sure Paul knew how great she felt for helping her fellow man (and not being selfish and traveling abroad like he'd done), he heard crackling noises coming from her cube.

"What are you doing?" Paul Instant Messaged Nicole.

"Nothing," Nicole replied quickly.

"It doesn't sound like nothing," Paul typed.

"Why don't you get back to work?!" she shot back.

Irritated, Paul returned his attention to his spreadsheet. A few seconds later, he heard "Mmmmm. Ohhhhhh. Mmmmm." Frustrated, he got up and marched over to Nicole's desk.

"What are you..." He stopped midstream, his mouth falling open in shock. "Are those my favorite peanut butter cookies you just opened and are eating?" he gasped.

"Hahaahaaaa! Yes! Yes! Yes!" Nicole moaned, thoroughly enjoying her cookiegasm.

"You know those are my favorite! Why didn't you just eat them while you were there? Why did you bring them back? Just to torture me?"

"Oh, I had some after I gave blood and, they were just so good, I had to bring another pack back with me," she retorted, and carried on with her torment. "Torturing you is just a bonus."

"Mmnt. I hate you," Paul responded flatly. "You know I'd give if I could." (See how the flat tone of Paul's Mmnt really conveyed his disgust with Nicole? We call this a teaching moment.)

"Sucks for you. Can you hand me my juice, please? I'm covered in cookie."

"Really, cookie whore? Really?" he said, dropping his head to the side and glaring at her. "I have work to do." Paul slunk back to his desk.

[NICOLE'S NOTE: *First, it's not what you're thinking. I'm not that kind of whore. I don't give it up like that but, if I did, honey, men would be lined up around the block, okay? Second, this type of whore is perfectly acceptable, and I freely embraced it that day. Keep reading—more to come on that later in the book.*]

"Wait!" Nicole called. "Come back a minute."

"No. It's too painful," Paul whined.

"Come here."

"What?" he barked, barely reappearing at the entrance of her cube.

Slowly, Nicole reached for the handle of her desk and opened it. Inside sat a bright, shiny red package of unopened peanut butter cookies. "For you," she offered.

"Really?" he said less defensively now. "You got them for me? You remembered?"

"Of course! I couldn't go and not get some for you. I know you love them. I just had to make you work for them," she laughed.

"Thank you, but you're still a cookie whore." He extended his hand in anticipation of the cookie blessing.

"Yes, yes I am," Nicole said, handing over the package and making the sign of the cross as she did so. "You may go now, my child."

Bowing, Paul laughed. "Thank you, my queen. You are both kind and generous." Paul returned to his desk. To this day, he maintains those were the best peanut butter cookies he ever had.

3. *APPROPRIATE MEN'S BATHROOM ETIQUETTE*

And now, on to the final and most important example of when "Mmnt!" is appropriate.

Let's talk for a minute about the men's bathroom. It should be a place to do your business, not the place you socialize and swap stories. When did it ever become okay or appropriate to smack a guy on the back and say hello when he is saddled up to a urinal in mid-pee? Don't you know that smacking someone on his back is a surefire way to break his concentration *and* his pee stream? Why even do it in the first place? What purpose does the touching of another man's back in the bathroom serve? Mmnt!

While we're on the subject, let's review appropriate men's bathroom etiquette. Assume there's a men's bathroom with three wall-mounted urinals and four stalls (see figure below).

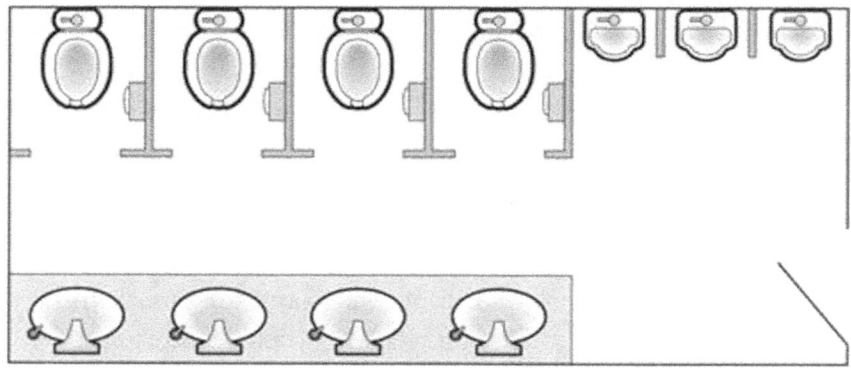

If you're the first guy in the bathroom and just need to pee, it is imperative you take one of the wall-mounted urinals in the corner. Never *ever* take the one in the middle. If you're the second guy in the bathroom and also just need to pee, then you take the other unoccupied corner urinal. This gives you a little privacy and ensures the smell from any flatulence you expel is minimized to that corner and not dispersed throughout the room. If, and only if, you are the third guy in the bathroom and there is no other choice, you may take the middle urinal (and even then, walk slowly, casually assessing the situation to see if anyone is near done and shaking; if they're shaking, walk even slower and cough to make your presence known so they know to hurry up). Honestly, they don't want to pee in front of an audience any more than you do.

[PAUL'S NOTE: *For those of you unfamiliar with shaking, it's the next-to-last step of the peeing process. When you're done peeing, you have to shake your pistol a little to ensure you don't drip once you re-holster. The final step is buckling your pants and/or zipping your fly.*]

[NICOLE'S NOTE: *If you're the type of guy who chooses to be at the middle urinal, one of two things is happening. Either you think you have the biggest package ever and are encouraging others to peek, or you en-joy holding your meat in the middle of a man sandwich. I'm not judging, though. Carry on.*]

[PAUL'S NOTE: *Don't be one of those guys at the corner urinal who takes forever to shake and zip up. It's just like the rules of a parking lot. Get in your car, turn it on and back out. Don't sit there forever and primp and prattle while others wait to pull into your space.*]

Similar rules apply to bathroom stall etiquette. If there are only three stalls, take a corner stall first unless one of them is a handicap stall. If there is a handicap stall, then you take that one first. A handicap stall is always preferred because there is more room to spread out, and sometimes you even have your own sink where you can wash up and quickly make an exit before any of your coworkers realize it was you who just stank up the whole place.

Other rules apply as well. If you're dropping a huge load of boys off at the pool, consider a courtesy flush or two. Don't keep sending them off the diving board without providing them some new water to swim in every once in a while. Mmnt!

[NICOLE'S NOTE: *Ditto for you girls, too!*]

A conversation at the sinks is fine when both of you are finished with your business and back on a level playing field. A conversation when one or both of you is midstream is not. What are you expecting? Eye contact? That will throw off the other person's aim. An intellectual exchange? All brain cells are concentrating on peeing and aiming. If you want dialogue, peeing will cease or reduce to a small trickle, thus causing a backup in available urinals and more people having to use the middle urinal. Hold that thought and say it at the sinks.

One last note for both men and women: do not, we repeat, do not talk on your cell phone while you're doing number one or number two. No one appreciates hearing your one-sided exchange, and the person on the other end surely doesn't want to know that's the kind of business you're conducting.

Mmnt! Yourself Into Infamy

Mmnt! is probably the one thing you can say that people will start to pick up subconsciously and not even know they've started using. When we started at our last company together, we would say "Mmnt!" during casual conversations with our new coworkers.

"The water in the faucet is brown. Where is the filtered water? Oh, that *is* the filtered water? Mmnt!"

"There's a meeting on Sunday, and we need to be there? Mmnt!"

"Your wife left you over the weekend and took all your money? Mmnt! Oh, and she left you with the kids? MMNT! And you have a strange itching sensation 'down there'? Double MMNT!" (And then slowly back away.)

[NICOLE'S NOTE: *TMI, people, TMI! Learn boundaries with your coworkers!*]

When we noticed the strange looks our coworkers were giving us, we explained the awesome power of "Mmnt!" and why we use it. Now we hear them using "Mmnt!" down the halls, around the corners, and in their own casual conversations.

"You're calling the Help Desk because you forgot your password…again? Mmnt. One moment, please."

"Mmnt! I don't know why that code isn't working!"

"You really expect me to believe you're late again because of traffic? You live three miles away. Mmnt!"

We're prouder than peacocks at how quickly "Mmnt!" has caught on. It's like verbal kudzu.

Trimming the Fat

There's always a time and place for saying what you feel, and knowing when that right time is will get you far in life. For those times when you can't express what you're truly feeling, a low-key "Mmnt" should get you through (and covertly indicate to those in the know that something funky just went down and you didn't like it one bit).

Embrace Your Bigness (EYB)

Meaning

Don't worry about your size or what others think about you. Be you, and be proud of who you are. Embrace your bigness! EYB!

Heart of the Story

Paul and his niece started this one. From a moment of hatefulness was born another empowering slogan, just like Hooves High, which allowed Paul to self-righteously declare he was big, loud, and proud!

Where "Hooves High" allows you to declare your love affair with food, EYB allows you to embrace who you are, regardless of size. EYB is more than just embracing your bigness when it comes to food, though. It's about embracing you and being comfortable with your size, whatever it is, and being proud of who you are. There are plenty of plus-size men and women out there who know how to work what the good Lord gave them.

Tail

Paul's niece, Rian (pronounced Ree-Ann), spends summers with Paul's family to make some extra money caring for Paul and Marilyn's three children. She's a lovely girl, very unassuming, good-natured, and sweet. Most days when the subject of dinner comes up, she just goes with the flow. If Paul or Marilyn is running late or there are lots of errands to run, she's fine with pizza, noodles, cereal—you name it.

Well, after a particularly stressful day with the children, she and Paul were going back and forth about that night's dinner menu. Paul wanted some comfort food, like his favorite Mama's Mac N' Cheese, or the cheesy, meaty, noodle goodness he calls Baked Ziti, but Rian wanted something healthier.

[PAUL'S NOTE: *Both of those dishes, by the way, are* great *for potlucks. I'll share them later in the book. Get your hooves high in anticipation!*]

Being a typical eighteen-year-old teenage girl, she was always looking for a low-carb or low-calorie option, which neither of these was.

[NICOLE'S NOTE: *And frankly, what does it even matter anyway? Your hips are gonna spread as you get older, no matter what you do. We say get a head start and beat old man time to it!*]

"How about some chicken on the grill?" she suggested.

Since there is no dessert that can be cooked on the grill, Paul has little use for it, and hence prefers not to associate with that appliance. Weary from his long workday, Paul said, "Do I really have to grill? Really? Can't we just have something easier? You're going to start growing feathers from all the chicken you eat!"

Unexpectedly, Rian sat up in the chair she'd been lounging in and exclaimed, "Why don't you just be quiet in all your bigness?!"

Mmnt!

After a stunned moment of silence, Paul stammered back, "Who are you talking to? Because I know it's not me!" Cue the neck roll.

Realizing what she'd said and recognizing that her Uncle Paul had not taken kindly to the "bigness" comment, she quickly back-pedaled and said, "I wasn't talking to you. I was talking to Ali."

Ali is Rian's older sister who also was visiting that week, and she was watching everything from the sidelines. With eyes big as saucers and putting on her best innocent bystander routine, she quickly retorted, "Umm, you weren't talking to me, Rian! I was just sitting here; don't drag me into this!" Then she walked off.

Alone, Rian and Paul faced off.

"How could you not have been talking to me? I'm the only other person in this conversation, Rian."

"I didn't mean it like that. I was really talking to Ali."

"Uh-huh. Well, why don't I, 'in all my bigness', just go into the kitchen and start making something that helps support that statement? We're having Mama's Mac 'n Cheese. Mmnt!" And with that, Paul turned, snout proudly in the air and hooves held high, and set forth finding all the ingredients to make his favorite dish to comfort his now battered esteem.

At dinner later that night, Paul recounted the story to Marilyn and the kids.

"So, I've just come home from an exceptionally rough day at work—you know the kind, hon," totally playing to Marilyn's sympathies, as she's a nurse and knows how it is to have a rough day with her patients. Score one for Paul.

Rian looked up from her plate of macaroni and twice-fried country-fried steak with gravy and waited.

Paul continued, "So, anyway, I'm just trying to get a feel for what everyone wants for dinner. I'm thinking we could all use some good old-fashioned southern comfort food, right? We've certainly had enough chicken lately." Paul shot a sideways glance to Rian to make sure she got the point. She returned his glance with the death stare. Score two for Paul.

"So, I'm throwing options out there, and Rian suggests grilled chicken. Again." Paul put heavy emphasis on "again" for effect. The point was made. "Now, we all know I love grilled chicken, but I am not the grill master. That's you, Mar, and I just didn't want to cook anything that wouldn't come close to your standards."

Marilyn smiled, pleased to be recognized for her grilling skills. Paul glanced sideways at Rian again and smiled, just a little. Death stare. Score three for Paul.

"I asked her to reconsider, and before I know it, she's spinning her head around like the little *Exorcist* girl…"

"Now wait just a minute," Rian interrupted. The kids started laughing.

"No, this is my story, and this is how I remember it, Ree, so just sit there and sulk," Paul said quickly. "So, her head is spinning, and she vomits this sentence on me: 'Just be quiet in all your bigness.' Can you believe that? She shushed me and she called me fat in one fell swoop!"

"I told you I was talking to Ali, Uncle Paul! It's just not like that, Aunt Pooh"--that's what she calls Marilyn—"you know I would never call Uncle Paul fat or tell him to be quiet! Mmnt!" With that, she put her fork down, crossed her arms, and the death stare turned to daggers. Score one for Rian for using "Mmnt!" appropriately. Score four for Paul for riling up the seemingly un-rilable (yes, that's a word, we're sure of it) child.

"Well," Paul said, "then she tries to drag Ali into it by saying she was telling *her* to be quiet in all her bigness."

"I know!" Ali interrupted. "Can you believe that? I was just sitting there watching the two of them go at it, and then Rian goes there with Uncle Paul." She looked over at Rian disapprovingly and added, "I was shocked," under her breath. Score one for Ali.

This was going brilliantly. Paul had never seen Rian this feisty before. It was hilarious. Reaching her boiling point, Rian put her palms down on the table and said, "Look, I just wanted some chicken. The kids were driving me crazy, and chicken is my comfort food. Ali, stop sitting there all innocent. You *know* I was talking to you because you're the one who always says you're big when you're really the size of a twig! I am done. D-O-N-E!"

Calmly, Paul looked over at Rian and said, "Rian, just embrace your bigness and eat the macaroni. We can have chicken tomorrow." Game, set, match!

Defeated, Rian picked her fork back up and took a hateful bite of the macaroni—you know, the kind of hateful where the fork hits the bottom of the plate just a little too hard in search of a cheesy pasta noodle. Secretly, Paul knew she loved it, though. Her hair was covering most of her face, but he could still see the tug of a smile at her lips.

Over the next couple of days, any time the subject of food, other than chicken or something else healthy, came up, Paul would exclaim "Just EYB!" Pretty soon, anytime someone in the family wanted a treat like ice cream with chocolate sauce or an extra yeast roll with dinner, the phrase was cried out by all.

It caught on at home so quickly that Paul decided to try it out at the office. He had his opportunity the very next week at lunch when he and Nicole were at their favorite pizza place.

"I am so fat. I have got to drop some weight," Nicole moaned as she continued to gnaw on her large slice of spinach, sun-dried tomato, beef, and extra-cheese pizza. "I want to be back in my cute clothes."

"You're not fat," Paul countered. "You just had a baby a few months back. Give yourself some time. You'll do it. However, that piece of pizza isn't helping."

"Really?" she deadpanned. "Thanks for that, but that baby is six months old now, and that excuse is getting old. Seriously, I'm turning into a fat ass! As Squeak said to Ms. Sophia in *The Color Purple*, I'm just 'a big, fat heffa.' That is so not cute!"

"Sorry, but you know what my new motto is?"

"Do tell," she inquired, still clearly perturbed Paul had called her out on her pizza slice.

"EYB."

"If you tell me that means 'exercise your butt' or 'eat yourself big', I'm gonna hurt you."

Snorts of laughter ensued, and Paul choked on his pretzel. A small piece may have even projected out of his mouth and onto the table, but we can't remember.

[NICOLE'S NOTE: *I remember fine, and it was more like pieces. One almost hit me. It was horrible! Chunks of dough were spewing everywhere, and I was like, "What the hell?" What a waste of a good piece of pretzel. Mmm…garlic and parmesan pretzels with Esperanza sauce. Mmm, soft doughy bread. Wait, sorry. I got distracted. Squirrel! LMAOPIMP!*]

When Paul recovered, he continued, still laughing, "No, stupid, it means 'embrace your bigness'. I came up with it last week, and it's great!"

Paul recounted the whole story.

"Don't you love it?" Paul beamed, as proud of his new creation as if he were just told the budget for a new dessert-only vending machine had been approved.

"That *is* cute. *Wait!* Did you just 'do a Rian' and call me fat? Are you saying I am *big?* Mmnt!"

"Well, yeah, but it's okay; just embrace who you are right now! You know what? Why don't you start rotating in a couple of your 'cute' clothes, as you call them? I'm sure they'll fit just fine."

"First off, I'm still tripping that you just Rianed me and called me fat on the sly. And second, uh, no."

"Truth hurts, sista! Just EYB! E-Y-B! No, seriously, how about that gold shirt you used to wear? You loved yourself in that."

"The gold cowl neck? The one we had all the bad luck in? Please, I tried that thing on a few weeks ago, and let's just say, as it was in Vegas, luck was not a lady that night!" she said.

"Oh my God. Was that what you wore on our Vegas trip?"

"Yes!"

[NICOLE'S NOTE: *Don't worry; we won't tease you with the Vegas story without telling it to you. You just have to wait a few chapters for it.*

"Hmm," Nicole thought about it. "I *have* lost a few pounds, mostly water weight, though." She laughed while finishing the rest of her pizza and casually refused the extra pretzel Paul was pointing to on his plate, contenting herself with her sweet tea for the remainder of the meal.

[NICOLE'S NOTE: *Because, after all, there are two types of drinks no good southern girl ever lets go to waste: alcohol and sweet tea.*]

A few days later, Paul eyed Nicole coming into work wearing her gold cowl neck. "Wow, look at you. That looks great!"

"I know. I am fabulous in it, aren't I?" she flounced. "I decided to just EYB, like you said. I'm a big girl right now, and that's that, so don't hate the jiggly! And when I started trying on some of my 'cute' clothes, they really did fit, so as far as I'm concerned, I am *back, baby!*" And with that, Nicole gave a little model-on-the-catwalk turn with a hint of Derek Zoolander's Magnum: puckered lips, sexy eyes, and sucked-in cheeks.

"EYB!" Paul cheered. "Now we need to go chat with the lard ass on the third floor that can't seem to keep his dunlap in check."

Intrigued and hoping for a new saying, Nicole asked, "What's a dunlap?"

"You know, that's what you call your belly when it's done lapped over your belt. A 'dunlap'."

Laughing, she replied, "Ohhh, I know exactly who you're talking about. Yeah, there has to be rules around EYB. You can embrace it, but you can't expose it! That's not cute! There are just certain things that need to be kept in check. Dunlaps and back rolls!"

How You, Too, Can EYB

Girls, nobody wants to see your rolls or be able to count them through your shirt. Oh, and while we're talking about 'girls', we're all for showing those off. Nicole is proud of her Nicolettes, but don't let them hang so low that your gigabits become gigaflops! Invest in a good cup holder, ladies. Yes, they are a bit more expensive than the ones you find in the discount store, but they really do wonders for your figure and your overall look.

[NICOLE'S NOTE: *You can also use the term "gigaflops" to describe that very busty coworker whose boobies have passed their prime but she won't admit it and keeps wearing shirts like they're still perky and full. Ladies, don't let this be you. Buy a first-rate over-the-shoulder boulder holder, please.*]

EYB for a woman is all about feeling comfortable in your skin. If you used to be a size six, and for whatever reason you're now a size sixteen and have been for more than a few years, EYB! You are what you are, and if you haven't lost those extra pounds by now, you probably won't anytime soon. So stop buying clothes from the frumpy chick's store, and EYB! Start wearing skirts again and show those big, beautiful legs. Let the "girls" loose a bit with a bright-colored shirt, and accessorize with a necklace that nestles between them, suggesting it's comfortable there <wink, wink>. *Sex in the City* it, girls, but just don't go overboard! Tight is not cute, because, trust us, there are plenty of people-watchers out there, like us, who will shake their heads with an under-the-breath "Mmnt, would you look at that? She knows she's wrong!" if you do.

Guys, if your gut hangs low, don't let it wobble to and fro. Cover that mess up. There is nothing worse than walking down the street and seeing another guy's dunlap hanging out below his shirt. There are plenty of great-looking and stylish shirts that can keep your chub in check. Don't fool yourself into thinking that if you wore a medium or large back in high school, you still can. Give those days up and recognize that, for most of us, things happen—like the freshman fifteen.

[PAUL'S NOTE: *For those of you living under a rock, the freshman fifteen is an unfortunate fifteen-pound curse that befalls both men and women once they go to college and their mamas aren't around to scrutinize what they're eating. You gain your independence, but you also gain your love handles (or "fatback" as we Southerners call it).*]

Once the freshman fifteen curse comes to pass, you graduate and get a job. Instead of twenty hours of classwork and study, you have a forty-hour-a-week job and less time to work out. Five more pounds. Then you get married and start spending your evenings having "quality" time together, giving you even less time to work out. Five more pounds. Oh, your wife is pregnant? Ten more sympathy pounds (per child). And finally, there's a little thing called aging that just seems to magically thicken your waist no matter what the hell you do to try to stop it.

[PAUL & NICOLE'S NOTE: *And we're not saying you should necessarily stop it. Sing it with us: "If you're happy and you're healthy, EYB!" <Clap! Clap!> "If you're happy and you're healthy, EYB!" <Clap! Clap!> "If you know you like to eat, then stomp your little feet. If you're happy and you're healthy, EYB!" <Clap! Clap!>*]

Just buy the right size and cover it up. Of course, some times are acceptable for showing up and showing off all your bigness —like the beach or the gym. Just make sure if you're at the beach that you're being appropriate. If your dunlap hangs down and hides your bikini bottom or Speedo from view, opt for a one-piece or for longer bathing trunks, please. We don't support sloppy. If you're embracing your bigness at the gym, find one that is fat-friendly and offers fellow Hoofers to work out with. There is nothing worse than joining a gym where everyone is already thin and beautiful.

One last thing for guys. If you do have a dunlap, that usually means you also have duncrack. You know, where your butt crack done starts to show whenever you sit down or bend over. Don't let this be you. Buy pants that are the right size and wear a belt that keeps them around your waist at all times. Duncrack is a surefire way to kill your chances at selling your pitch during a meeting (or having your way with the office resource hog).

[PAUL'S NOTE: *Oh, yes: the office resource hog. This is one of our favorites, and we always spend the first few weeks at any new job searching for the resource hogs. They are, quite simply, the office sluts. You know, the men or women who seem to get more ass than a toilet seat! They have a second career doing the bowlegged cha-cha with as many of their coworkers as possible. Once you've identified them, make friends with them. They're getting more than a good time during their trysts. They're also getting all the good gossip, so if you want to know whose wheels to grease on the job, find out who they're greasing first!*]

Take Paul's friend, Tyler. After hearing about EYB, he recounted this story for us. Back in the early 1990s, he was a young guy in his twenties. He, like so many other guys, joined a fraternity in college and hadn't really monitored his diet. He'd EYBed on pizza and beer.

As a result, his athletic physique had given way to a slightly rounder belly (a "kegger", his fraternity brothers nicknamed it) and, although it was a source of great pride for him, he hadn't really thought about how his dunlap changed the way his clothes fit.

After Tyler graduated, he was snapped up by a large software firm and sent to a conference to sell potential customers on their latest suite of products. In preparation for the big event, he ventured to the mall and bought a couple of trendy suits in the same size he'd always worn. No need to try them on, right? Unfortunately, the pant style at the time was a clean, beltless look.

[PAUL'S NOTE: *You see where this is going, right?*]

On the first day of the conference, during his first presentation, Tyler's computer monitor went black. Wanting to quickly resolve the issue and not lose his audience (because if it's one thing IT people are, it's impatient), the first thing he checked was the connection from the monitor to the PC. Because the PC was on the floor, he bent over to check the connection. When he did, the back of his shirt rode up and his fashion-forward beltless pants went fashion-backward, exposing his duncrack.

[PAUL'S NOTE: *When Tyler bent over, it also revealed an embarrassing "Kiss This" tattoo, complete with a pair of cherry red lips, that his fraternity brothers had convinced him was cool. He wasn't sure at first but, in his drunken state, was easily convinced. ROFLPIMP!*]

What do you think happened when Tyler exposed his duncrack? Simultaneously, everyone in the audience stopped thinking about the features his company's new software suite could offer them, and they became fixated on his pasty white butt crack (oh, and his unfortunate ink—LOL!). Even though he restored power to the monitor quickly, no one cared when he began his presentation again. His shirt was disheveled and hanging out, and he'd just assaulted the entire audience with his butt cleavage. No one stayed to get more information after he finished, but Tyler felt sure they enjoyed it due to all the smiles he saw in the audience.

When he returned from the conference in Florida, his boss called him into his office.

"Guess what I have in my hand?" his boss said, neatly fanning a stack of papers out in front of Tyler.

"I don't know, Jim. What?" Tyler asked.

"Comment cards from your presentations. Most of them were really good." He paused, looking down from the bridge of his nose. "However, there are a few from one of your demos that have me concerned."

"Really? I thought they all went great," Tyler said, a little confused. "We had a lot of interest in our products, and I even lined up presales for a few of our existing customers."

"Yes, you did. It wasn't about the way the information was presented or the amount of presales you had. It's about your appearance."

"My appearance? I was dressed in a suit all three days."

"Did it fit?" Jim asked.

"What do you mean, 'Did it fit?'" Tyler said mockingly, a bit agitated. "Of course it did! It's not like I was down there flashing them my chest or anything."

"According to these, it was another part of your body you were flashing."

"What?"

"Did you have an incident with your monitor?" Jim continued.

"Yeah, but it was just a loose connection. I had it fixed in less than a minute," Tyler said, confused.

"Well apparently, when you went to fix it, you flashed more than your chest. You flashed them your rear end."

"Oh," Tyler responded, somewhat sheepishly now. "Let me see those comment cards."

Jim handed them over.

"Wow! 'Presenter was knowledgeable, but had a hiccup with the monitor. When he went to fix it, he flashed us his backside, including a cute little lips tattoo. I'd suggest he buy some clothes that fit next time.' 'The product looks good, but seeing your butt crack was not.' 'Next time, please wear clothes that aren't so tight.' Ouch. Sorry, Jim, I didn't even realize I'd done that."

"Let's be honest, Ty. You're great with people, and I know you like to look good, but you're a big guy. You need to buy some clothes that fit you better. Your belly button is distracting me with a peep show right now," Jim said with a chuckle.

Embarrassed, Tyler quickly sucked in his stomach, retreating his little dancer back behind her curtain. "Sorry, Jim. It won't happen again—the belly button or the presentation snafu."

"I know it won't, and I'm just telling you as a friend and as someone else who had his own fair share of peep shows when he was first starting. One more thing, though, before you go."

"What?" Tyler replied, looking up at Jim, still somewhat embarrassed.

"You have a tattoo of some lips on your butt?"

Laughing, "Uh, yeah. Long story. Big mistake. No further comment." Not wanting to sustain further humiliation, Tyler hastily retreated from Jim's office that day, but he took away three important lessons from their meeting:

1. Always bend at the knees.
2. Buy clothes that fit and won't leave you exposed should you have an ill-fated need to throw your ass in the air and check on something.
3. Don't ever let your frat brother talk you into getting any sort of tattoo on your cheeks. Any of your cheeks.

Just remember, friends don't let friends dunlap or duncrack. Dress responsibly.

Trimming the Fat

Be comfortable with yourself. When you're not, your guard is always up and you're constantly worrying about what others are thinking. When you are comfortable with yourself, people are automatically drawn to you and want to be around you. This is important no matter where you are because it helps alleviate tension, distrust, and uncertainty. So, EYB (whatever your size), and watch the relationships build!

Mondo!

Meaning

Get my ass outta this situation—now!

Heart of the Story

This one comes from our good friend, Tina, who taught us this phrase.

Before we tell you the tail, we need to tell you about Tina. She is one of our dearest friends and was one of the first people to introduce herself to us at our last job. She's a petite blonde in her very young fifties, and she has great taste in clothes and jewelry. When it comes to jewelry, her motto is 'the bigger, the better'. She has this one pearl ring that damn near covers her whole finger, and Nicole covets it.

[NICOLE'S NOTE: *Yes, yes I do!*]

Perhaps when she reads that we called her "petite" and "very young", she'll be so distracted basking in her glory that Nicole can pry it away from her. Anyway, she came bopping over (yes, she bops, not walks) and said, all in one breath, "Hi, I'm Tina! Welcome! I am so glad you're here. I can already tell I'm going to like you. It's a shame you don't work for me because I'm fabulous, but don't worry; I'll teach you everything you need to know. Like, if you ever hear me say I have 'anal glaucoma', it means I can't see my ass coming into the office that day; just keep that in mind." She smiled wildly through her retro, black, cat-eyed glasses and took a breath. That is when we knew it was acceptable to speak.

Anyone who introduces us to new and clever catchphrases is instantly our friend, but she introduced us to "anal glaucoma" in the first thirty seconds without even knowing what we were about, so that made her an instant dear friend and a kindred spirit.

[PAUL'S NOTE: *Plus, she fully supports and endorses our semi-famous potluck bonanzas.*]

Many of our favorite moments and catchphrases were influenced by Tina. There are even a few catchphrases that were hilarious and made us LMAOPIMP, but we were too afraid to print them. If you ever see us in person, ask us about "FF".

Tail

"Mondo!" was a Tina-ism truly born out of necessity. The first few days and weeks on a new job are always the same. It's like high school all over again: finding the right clique, identifying the right lunch table, etc. You spend a lot of time taking it all in, trying to look cool and not at all desperate, all the while secretively looking for your new best work friend. And just like high school, there are always cliques you don't fit in with and characters that immediately set off your Spidey senses and scream, "Danger, Will Robinson, danger!" As it always happens, those people are the ones who want to introduce themselves to you right off, in hopes that you'll somehow find them endearing and become their new best friend.

This was one of those days. It started off fine, and Nicole was in a really good mood. In her usual attempts to brighten everyone else's day (at her last job, she was dubbed "Sunshine"), Nicole went around checking in on her peeps and spreading the rays. Of course, Tina was always on that stop because, together, their rays of sunshine could light up even a black hole.

[PAUL'S NOTE: *When they're together, it's like sunbathing at Panama City Beach at 10:30 in the morning. You can only take a little because the rays are so bright you're bound to get burned in the first fifteen minutes.*]

Now most times, when you see that person everyone in the office typically avoids, you quickly walk the other way or look too busy to acknowledge his or her presence. You know, give off the impression you're so deep in thought you don't see the person, quite intentionally unintentionally. Unfortunately, Nicole doesn't quite get this concept and smiles at everyone. *Everyone!*

[NICOLE'S NOTE: *Old school southern girl that I am, I believe everyone should have "a Coke and smile!" Like the Equal Employment Opportunity Commission, I don't discriminate.*]

So, of course, it was only a matter of time before Nicole was introduced to Jeffrey, the office creeper. You know, the person who weirds out everyone. As Nicole stood at Tina's desk that morning, chatting, laughing, and spreading her sunshine, she looked up at a most inopportune time.

Jeffrey was rounding the corner and noticed the energy in the air. Wanting to be a part of the fun, he walked right over. The problem with this encounter was that Tina's cube was in the corner, with only one way in and one way out. Not recognizing the warning Tina was giving—a combination of disturbing eye twitches and head nods—Nicole simply smiled her normal, inviting smile.

"Hello," Jeffrey said, making contact.

"Hey, sweetie," Nicole replied, seeing the face of someone she hadn't met yet.

[PAUL'S NOTE: *Nicole doesn't care if she knows you or not. Everyone is a "sweetie" until they piss her off. Then they're a sonofabitch. One word, not four, said quickly and forcefully.*]

"I've been watching you for the last week, walking about and meeting everyone, and every time I see you, you've reminded me of someone. I just didn't know who until now." His eyes remained fixed and unblinking on hers. Nicole momentarily glanced at Tina and caught a strange deer-in-the-headlights look from her.

Ignoring Tina and his comment about "watching" her for a week, Nicole continued, flattered, "Really? WOW!" In her mind, she was running down the list of actresses she pictured herself looking like. Perhaps a young Vanessa Williams. They had the same cocoa-colored skin, hair, and eye color. Yeah, she'd gotten that a lot. Perhaps Nicole Ari Parker, Mariah Carey, or one of the countless other café au laits because, frankly, as she pondered and giggled to herself, "They (as in all non-café au laits) all think we look alike." She fanned her eyelashes in anticipation of the compliment.

"The Oracle," he said in his flat, monotone voice. Still no blinking.

Nicole processed the comment. Finally, after a second or two, she stammered, a little higher pitched than before, "From *The Matrix*?" Tina covered her mouth and barely stifled a laugh. Nicole did a half neck roll and stayed cocked back at ninety degrees, ready to finish the movement if he agreed with her.

"Yes! You've seen it, too!" He brightened. Blink.

Full neck roll. "I've seen it, and I remind you of her? Really?"

"I'm sure it's just because you both have the same hair," Tina interjected, realizing the sting of his comment and trying to minimize the carnage that could ensue from Nicole.

[NICOLE'S NOTE: *Girls, we understand these things, don't we?*]

Tina also had office seniority on her side and knew that Jeffrey was just one failed "hello" from going postal. "You know, it's curly and beautiful," she sing-songed, trying to appease both parties and frantically looking around for backup.

Temporarily distracted by Tina from inwardly pondering the different ways to kill this person she'd just met, there was a lull that allowed Jeffrey to continue. "Yours isn't white like hers, but yes, that's it. They're the same!" He brightened even more.

Silence.

"Wow. Well, I've never heard that one before. Hmmm. Yeah, I guess I could see how I would remind you of her with my current haircut."

At this point, Nicole realized something was not quite right with this dude, and the best thing was to allow him to be on his merry little way. After all, her new cut was *nothing* like the Oracle's. Not at all. No, Nicole's new haircut was reminiscent of Lonette McKee in *Jungle Fever*: sassy with attitude. Though, she thought momentarily, the Oracle's hair was kind of sassy, and she really wasn't too bad for an older woman. Still, Jeffrey *had* just said she looked like a sixty-something-year-old woman. Yes, Jeffrey was off the Christmas surprise list.

"Well, I *am* all-knowing," Nicole said, trying to save face a bit and somehow turn this case of simple battery into a victim's survivor story.

[NICOLE'S NOTE: *The positive from the negative, right?*]

Jeffrey blinked. Smile.

Awkward silence from Tina and Nicole.

"Umm, I guess I should get back to work now," Nicole said, attempting to hide her disdain for the sonofabitch and hoping he would catch a clue and move on. She then turned to Tina, gave her the "follow me" look, and added, "Thanks for stopping by and sharing." Then she headed back towards her cube.

Once Jeffrey was gone, Tina caught up with Nicole, and the two of them beat a hot foot over to Paul. Grateful for the distraction, Paul looked up, anxious to hear about their latest escapade.

"Let me tell you what just happened," Nicole blurted with a full neck roll, squinted eyes, and hands on hips.

At that moment, Tina could no longer compose herself and burst out laughing. The piercing evil eye that Nicole hurled at Tina to shut her up backfired, and Tina fell to the floor convulsing, complete with snorts and all. The throaty "Mmnt!" Nicole responded with didn't help either.

Ignoring Tina, Nicole continued, still cocked sideways from her neck roll. "As I was saying, I'm over there minding my own business, talking to Tina, when Jeffrey walked up. Do you know who I'm talking about?"

"Oh yeah, I know Jeffrey. He's a little weird. He accosted me one day when we were in the break room. He's a member of some card-playing group, and when I went to get a packet of tea, he grabbed them first and, in one motion, fanned them out to me with a 'ta-da' flair. *Weird!*"

"Mmnt! Then you know where I'm going with this already. Can you believe he just told me I look like the Oracle?"

Second neck roll; shift of hip.

"You mean the black chick who is seventy years old and smokes in every scene of *The Matrix*? You remind him of *her*?" Paul's shocked look mirrored Nicole's attitude, not at all like the betrayal displayed by the laughing hyena behind her.

[PAUL'S NOTE: *Not yet at least.*]

Paul sympathized and said, "He just came up and said that to you? I can't believe that. Who would do that? What was he thinking?"

"He wasn't thinking. That's the point. He must just be off. The Oracle. Really?" Nicole replied, flabbergasted.

"Well, at least you look young for your age," Tina cried out.

Turning to face Tina, who was still on floor, Nicole looked her dead in the eye and said in her hoodest of tones, "A bitch 'bout to get cut."

[PAUL'S NOTE: *That's "ghetto" for those of you who don't understand "hood."*]

Continued laughter. Nicole made a mental note to possibly scratch Tina off the Christmas surprise list as well.

Unable to control himself, Paul turned Tina's stray dog into a pack and began howling. After a minute of Nicole still not joining in, and knowing about her "hood" tendencies, he tried to reel the situation back in.

"Well, it is kind of funny, Nic. I'm sure he didn't mean it as an insult. I mean, he is a little different, but I think he just wanted to talk to you and didn't know what else to say."

"*Whatever!*" huffed Nicole.

"No, really. I think that's it, too," Tina chimed in, finally simmering down. "He's really a nice guy. I'm sure Paul's right."

Nicole let out a final "*Whatever*" and flopped down in her chair, leaving the cackling hyenas alone at Paul's desk to continue their wheezing. She made another mental note that if she was the Oracle, she would use her mental abilities to make Tina and Paul choke on one of their asthmatic cackles.

A few minutes later, Tina began to realize that being called an eighty-year-old woman isn't a good thing when you're in your thirties, and she told Paul to walk over to Nicole's cube with her.

[NICOLE'S NOTE: *Yes, the Oracle's age continues to go up as this story goes on. It mirrors my agitation about the whole situation!*]

Approaching hesitantly, Tina said, "You know what, Nicole? It really wasn't the best of situations. We were trapped. We should have used a Mondo!"

Nicole turned around in her chair and glared at Tina. Paul gave Tina the sign to speak quickly or be ready to dodge a knife.

"'Mondo!' is the safe word my little gay boyfriend and I use when we're in situations we need help getting out of," she explained.

Nicole's hostility instantly turned to interest as neither she nor Paul knew where to begin. They weren't sure what frightened them more: the fact Tina had a little gay boyfriend they hadn't heard about or that Tina and her little gay boyfriend had a safe word. They edged closer to ensure they heard every word.

Tina continued, "'Mondo!' is what you say when you're in a situation and you need rescuing. Like, if Paul knew about Mondo! I could have sent him an instant message that simply said, 'MONDO!' He would have known it was his cue to come over and make up some excuse that would have freed us from our hostile environment. It could have been something like 'Hey, you two ready for our meeting?' or 'Hey, I need you guys for a second to help us with this project' and that would have given us the out we needed. Understand?"

At that moment, the power of Mondo! had been bestowed upon Paul and Nicole. They saw it for its good and simply nodded, bowing to its power. Yes, Tina and her little gay boyfriend were on to something, and now Paul and Nicole had the power as well.

But with all that power came the caveat. Tina, in her most Glinda the Good Witch of Oz voices, whispered, "But you must be careful when to use Mondo! and whom you use it around. You can't just blurt it out in front of someone. You have to say it in a way that the person being Mondo!d doesn't catch on."

In awe of their mentor, Tina, the new office Oz, they didn't make a sound—just gave a head nod to convey their understanding and reverence.

St. Patrick's Day came just a few weeks later. Paul and Nicole decorated their areas with St. Patty's Day decor and were in the spirit. Paul perched a tall, green-and-white-striped hat on one corner of his cube, and Nicole posted a sign declaring her affinity for drinking and being able to keep up with the best Irish drinker proudly displayed under her name tag.

As tradition had it, Paul came in on Saint Patrick's Day wearing a green shirt. Nicole, however, always defying convention, wore a green shot glass around her neck like a necklace and dared anyone to point out the HR implications of supporting alcohol in the workforce.

[NICOLE'S NOTE: *Bring on the Patrón, baby!*]

The day seemed to be going well. The mood was fun, a happy energy filled the air, and Paul's step had an extra bounce to it.

After drinking his first bottle of water that morning, it was time for Paul to take a bio break.

[PAUL'S NOTE: *That's the business phrase for 'I have to pee.'*]

[NICOLE'S NOTE: We *firmly believe the more water you drink, the more it dilutes the calories and fat you eat and helps to flush them before they stick, so drink lots of it.*]

Upon entering the bathroom, guess who was waiting to accost Paul? Jeffrey. Before Paul could even assess the stall situation and apply appropriate men's bathroom etiquette, Jeffrey was upon him.

"Look at you," he said.

"And? Is something wrong?" Paul asked hesitantly.

"You're wearing green today."

"Right. It's St. Patrick's Day. I'm in the spirit." Not knowing where this was going, Paul began scanning the stalls looking for feet in case he needed to call out for help.

"You know who you remind me of?"

Oh Jesus, Paul deliberated in his head, remembering Nicole's encounter a few weeks earlier. "Um, who?"

"I can't remember his name."

Brilliant, Paul thought, rolling his eyes.

"You know, the big guy in the cartoon who loves the big girl, and they have little monsters together in the last one."

"What?" Paul uttered, amazed he was even having this conversation. "A cartoon about big people having baby monsters."

"It's a comedy. They live in the swamp; it was a huge movie," he blinked. Smile.

"You mean *Shrek*?"

"Yes, you remind me of Shrek!" Blink. "Have you seen it?" Blink. Blink.

"Uh, yeah, I've seen it several times…with my kids. I'm just not sure I identified with the fat ogre who lived in the swamp."

"No, no, I didn't mean it like that. With that shirt you have on today, you're both just big and green."

"That helps," Paul responded flatly. "I didn't even know you had kids, Jeffrey."

"I don't."

"Okay then," Paul said quickly. "Well, Shrek has to pee, so let me get to it."

"Okay." Blink.

Paul awkwardly stepped around Jeffrey to get to an empty stall, shaking his head back and forth, having an Etch-A-Sketch moment.

"Have a good day," Paul called over his shoulder, hoping to allay any postal tendencies that could be boiling to the surface.

[PAUL'S NOTE: *For those of you unfamiliar with an Etch-A-Sketch moment, it's when you shake your head back and forth trying to erase a vivid mental image someone has painted for you, just like how you shake an Etch-A-Sketch to erase it.*]

After Paul's bio break, he burned a hot foot over to Nicole and fiercely whispered, "Mondo!"

"What happened?!" Nicole jumped, hearing the secret word and instantly going on the lookout for the offender.

"Jeffrey."

"Oh no! Where?" she whispered, looking around.

"It's over now. I was trapped. Call Tina, though. You both have to hear this. Tell her 'Mondo!'"

Nicole spun back around in her chair and quickly typed "Mondo!" into Tina's instant message window. Tina appeared within seconds, glasses half-cocked on her face and her blonde hair disheveled. Eying the situation and looking for the Mondo! victim, she slowed down.

"Hi, guys," she said apprehensively, casting a wide glance at the people around them.

"No, it's okay now," Paul shuddered. "I needed to use Mondo! but I was trapped in the bathroom with Jeffrey and couldn't, so I need to use it now...retroactively."

"That's a new twist on the rule," Tina considered for a moment, "but I'll allow it. Tell us what happened." She hopped up on Nicole's desk, using it as her makeshift throne, and prepared for the story.

"Well, I guess there's good news and there's bad news," Paul pondered. "The good news is I wasn't called an eighty-year-old Oracle."

Cue the giggling.

"The bad news is I was called another character from a movie."

"No way! Who?" Nicole gasped.

"Get ready for it," Paul prepared them, pausing just a moment for effect. Nicole and Tina moved to the edge of their chair and throne.

"Shrek!" he finally revealed.

Giggling turned to guffaws.

"He said it's because we're both big and green!"

Guffaws turned into full-blown fits of laughter.

"*No way!*" Tina oinked between snorts.

"Well, at least I stayed black and didn't turn another color. You were wronged," Nicole empathized.

"I know! Plus, you know my rule! I hate talking in the bathroom."

"Wait, I'm a little upset now," Tina said, her laughter turning to a pout. "Jeffrey's known me for years and never once said I reminded him of anyone famous. I'm going to have to talk to him about that. You wait."

"Really?" Paul and Nicole said jointly.

"Like an old black woman or a fat green monster?" Paul added.

"Really!" Tina insisted, clearly upset.

Paul thought for a minute. "Fine. You can be Ouiser. How's that?" He smiled. "We can have the Oracle, Shrek, and Ousier."

"Shirley McClaine's character in *Steel Magnolias*?" Tina scoffed.

"That's perfect!" Nicole agreed. "She's a wise ass full of wisdom, sarcasm, and snarky humor, all mixed together to make up one fabulous woman."

"Oh, I like that," Tina cheered.

"Wait a minute!" Nicole interjected. "Ouiser *is* kinda cool and not at all like being called an eighty-year-old, wrinkly, chain-smokin' black woman or an ogre. Mmnt!"

Looking at the clock and remembering he had a meeting coming up, Shrek ended their impromptu assembly. "Well, thanks for letting me recount my much needed Mondo! story, but I have to get back to work."

"Yes, I'm sure it's safe now," the Oracle predicted, and she returned to her e-mail.

"Y'all take care, bitches," Ouiser added as she dismounted from her throne and headed back to her subjects.

Secret Mondo Non-Verbal Cue

Obviously, there are times when you can't just scream "Mondo!", especially when the assailant is within earshot or, God forbid, talking directly to you...alone. For those times, we decided we needed a secret nonverbal cue to notify any of our in-the-know friends to save us.

The trick is in the eyebrow. If you're standing, you want to simply run your finger along the perimeter of your eyebrow as if you're scratching an itch or smoothing down an errant brow hair. When sitting at a table, it's easy to just put your hand on your chin like you're listening intently and then, ever so slightly, just lift one finger and run it along your eyebrow. It's totally unnoticeable to the offender because it looks like one of the many common, unconscious moves we make each day, like crossing our legs.

To those in the know, though, that subtle move will be a desperate call to action to come to your aid, help you end the conversation and get you back to safety with your sanity intact. However, if your signs go unanswered, do not go into Mondo! paranoia. You should not begin rubbing your eye as if it's record on a DJ's table. Again, we should state this is a subtle movement.

If you see a fellow Mondotian in need of assistance, don't, we repeat don't, leave them stranded! If you do, the *Curse of a Thousand Doughnuts* will befall you, and no one will be there to proclaim "Hooves High" or "EYB" with you. And while a thousand doughnuts may sound good in theory, you'll change your mind when your ass magically spreads as quickly as a Popsicle melting on a sidewalk in the hot Arizona sun and your lonely hooves are there without a friend to get your lardaceous rump on the treadmill. Mmnt!

Trimming the Fat

Keep your eyes peeled and your ears open to help your fellow friends and coworkers out of sticky situations. Find the right "Mondo!" partner (because you can't "Mondo!" with just anybody), and make sure the offender doesn't realize they're being Mondo!d. That's a surefire way to destroy a relationship (and lose a potluck peep).

ROFLWMM

Meaning

Rolling on the floor laughing, wiping my mascara.

Heart of the Story

Ladies, we've all been there! Someone tells a funny story, your eyes start to water from laughing so hard and, before you know it, you're blotting like crazy, trying to keep your mascara from running into your eyes and down your face. Yes, you're wiping your mascara! Now you might be saying to yourself, "Nicole, they do make waterproof mascara; just wear that." True, they do, but have you tried to get that crap off? MMNT! It doesn't come off with mere water (helloooo, waterproof!), which means you have to use soap. *Soap*...on the eyes? IDTS (I don't think so)! And yes, they do make mascara remover, but really? I'm already paying eight dollars for mascara, and then I have to pay another fifteen dollars for the remover? That's twenty-three dollars for freakin' mascara. MMNT! IDTS! Regular is just fine!

[NICOLE'S NOTE: *Ladies, laughter feeds the soul and puts a smile on your face, but you also don't want it to leave two black rings around your eyes like you've been knocked out, so always keep a compact with you. If you don't have a compact, use the selfie feature on your phone.*]

Tail

Sometimes things spiral out of control, and you are powerless to stop them. Such is the case with the tail of Lambie. What started out as a humorous tactic to try to ease a teammate into a better communication style, turned into something far more elaborate and twisted.

Ann had been a member of Paul's team for only a few short months. She'd been with the company for a long time, knew everyone and everything, and was responsible for the security administration process (i.e. assigning new IDs and passwords, creating e-mail addresses, and just generally keeping everyone in line). She was excellent in every aspect of her job but one: communication.

It's not that Ann didn't know how to communicate well with people or wasn't capable of writing profound documents. She was, but to her, most people were just stupid and not worth her time. She had a one-strike rule. The first time you messed up, she was nice, taking the time to explain the infraction and instructing you on how not to do it the next time. If you messed up again, you were dead to her and her communication style turned brisk and to the point. Now you're probably saying to yourself, "Well, what's so bad about that? Those dumbasses had a chance."

The problem was Paul. His philosophy is that the customer is king, and even when the customer is wrong, you continue to be nice. Paul was well-known throughout the organization as the "velvet hammer". He could convince you to do something or change your behavior without you even knowing he was doing it. He coined the phrase "being fluffy" and he spent a lot of time convincing his team that they needed to learn the art of being fluffy.

Most people on his team converted willingly. Some were a bit more challenging, regressing a time or two but, in the end, Paul's way won out and they came over to the fluffy side. Ann proved more difficult. Her feet were firmly planted on the dark side and, no matter how much sunshine or fluffiness he pumped into it, the darkness engulfed it, chewed it up, and spit it back out, crowing the whole time.

Not one to give up easily, Paul saw something at the store he thought might finally convince Ann, or at least help remind her, to be fluffy. It was a Lambie, a cute little stuffed lamb. Who epitomized fluffy more than Lambie, with her sweet little white fur, long black eyelashes, and cute little smile? He quickly bought her, took her home, and tied a little bow around her neck with a note to remind Ann to be fluffy.

After lunch the next day, Paul sat in his office, pleased that Ann had accepted Lambie with nary a discouraging word or outburst. While enjoying some celebratory chocolate cake, he suddenly heard shrieks of hysteria coming from Ann's direction. By the time Paul got to her desk, a large crowd had assembled.

"Is everything okay?" Paul asked. "Where's Ann?"

"She's not here," came a reply, "but she left you something."

Oh no, Paul thought. He asked, "What is it?"

"See for yourself." The crowd parted, giving Paul a complete view of the scene. Aghast, he turned away quickly. It was full-on child abuse. Lambie had been strung up by her little neck and hung from the under-the-shelf lighting of her cube. Ann had even taken the time to arrange Lambie's tongue so it was hanging to the side.

Nicole, clearly pleased at Ann's antics, tapped Paul on the shoulder. "I guess your plan didn't work, huh?"

"Shut up. This isn't over. Let me think."

"Let's take her into protective custody, just like child protective services would do," came a strong female voice from the back of the crowd.

"Yeah, do it!" others chimed in.

"What?" Paul said.

"Untie her and take her away from Ann. She's not a fit mother to this poor little lamb."

"And then what do we do?" Paul asked.

"We make her feel bad," came Nicole's sinister voice as she looked around at her fellow conspirators. A plan was hatched.

As Nicole and her self-appointed DFACS team untied Lambie's noose and liberated her from her abusive home, they worked out the details. First, they would create an e-mail account in Lambie's name, and then they would begin a series of e-mails explaining to Ann how she'd abused her poor little lamb, copying all the process teams to maximize the guilt level. Ann could get Lambie back, but she was going to be sentenced to community service, which included performing "fluffy" acts that were customer service-oriented.

Best laid plans and all. Below are the actual e-mails, in chronological order, as they happened over the next month. Every process team joined in on the mayhem, and what ensued was a hilarious, and often surprising, example of how eight groups came together, bonded, and became the strongest team in the company-- once it was all over.

One thing to note. Ann was married to Carlos, and even though they were on two separate teams, they both reported to Paul, so Carlos was seeing the abuse his wife was taking for Lambie. He was a very straitlaced character with a military background, so when you get to the part where Carlos gets involved, keep that in mind.

From: Lambie
Sent: Monday, February 11, 2008 8:52 AM
To: Ann
Cc: All Process Teams
Subject: Lambie's Whereabouts
Dear Mommy,
WHHYYYYYYYYYYY!!!!!!!!!!

On Friday, some people came to our cube and said you were a neglectful mommy and that they had to take me away. **I Don't Understand.** I thought our cube was just fine. They said you were abusive to me and that it was wrong to string me up by my neck. I explained that this is normal. Don't all kids live like this? They were VERY upset with you and said you were unfit to raise me. They said I will go live with a foster family. Mommy...Who are the Fosters?!!!

I'm so sad without you. I know you love me. PLEEEEAAASSSSEEEE SAVE ME FROM THE DFACS PEOPLE. HEEELLLLLPPPPP!!!!!
Love,
Your Adorable Lambie

From: Ann
Sent: Monday, February 11, 2008 8:54 AM
To: Lambie
Cc: All Process Teams
Subject: RE: Lambie's Whereabouts
Never fear, wee fluffy one. I shall save you!

From: Lambie
Sent: Tuesday, February 12, 2008 3:23 PM
To: Ann
Cc: All Process Teams
Subject: Running Away
Hi Mommy,
I ran away earlier today and tried to call you but your TREO doesn't have voicemail set up and I wasn't able to leave a message.

The DFACS people caught up with me, though, and brought me back. They keep talking about the Foster family. I'm scared, Mommy.

Missing You,
Lambie

From: Ann
Sent: Wednesday, February 13, 2008 7:33 AM
To: Lambie
Cc: All Process Teams
Subject: RE: Running Away

Dear Lambie-poo,
Don't forget the training I gave you on ChopFu. The next time those DFACS pillocks aren't looking, use the Sleeping Chop of Destruction maneuver and make a break for it! Mummy's so sorry that her voice mail does not work—her bosses can't seem to raise the lolly for a phone with functioning messaging services.

Never fear, we will be reunited!
Ann

From: Release Management
Sent: Wednesday, February 13, 2008 8:11 AM
To: Ann; Lambie
Cc: All Process Teams
Subject: RE: Running Away

What's a pillock? Is it a very tiny pill? Or something you use to lock up very tiny pills?

From: Security
Sent: Wednesday, February 13, 2008 8:24 AM
To: Ann; Lambie

Cc: All Process Teams
Subject: RE: Running Away

A pillock is the same as a plonker.

From: Asset Management
Sent: Wednesday, February 13, 2008 8:26 AM
To: Ann; Lambie
Cc: All Process Teams
Subject: RE: Running Away

And what in the world is a "plonker"?

From: Security Administration
Sent: Wednesday, February 13, 2008 8:28 AM
To: Ann; Lambie
Cc: All Process Teams
Subject: RE: Running Away

same as a wassock

From: Desktop Services
Sent: Wednesday, February 13, 2008 8:33 AM
To: Ann; Lambie
Cc: All Process Teams
Subject: RE: Running Away

same as a wassup!!!

From: Provisioning
Sent: Wednesday, February 13, 2008 8:43 AM
To: Ann; Lambie

Cc: All Process Teams
Subject: RE: Running Away

pillock

(slang, very mildly derogatory) foolish person, used esp. in northern England but also common elsewhere.

From: Ann
Sent: Wednesday, February 13, 2008 08:45 AM
To: Lambie
Cc: All Process Teams
Subject: RE: Running Away

I'm so happy that my second child's misery is generating such illuminating and educational discourse…[sob!]

Heartbroken,

Ann

From: Release Management
Sent: Wednesday, February 13, 2008 8:55 AM
To: Ann; Lambie
Cc: All Process Teams
Subject: RE: Running Away

Hey, can we all be a little more sympathetic to Ann's situation? Has anyone even offered to help her get Lambie back?

Ann, if there is anything I can do, just let me know.

BTW, I saw the movie *The Negotiator* twice—if that means anything to you.

From: Ann
Sent: Wednesday, February 13, 2008 8:56 AM
To: Release Management
Cc: All Process Teams
Subject: RE: Running Away

Thank you, kind sir. Please don't ask for proof of life—I couldn't stand it if DFACS sent back a hoof or eyebrow. [sniffle, sob!]

From: Carlos
Sent: Wednesday, February 13, 2008 8:59 AM
To: Ann; Lambie
Cc: All Process Teams
Subject: RE: Running Away
Dear LC,
I got your message and have assembled an extraction team. The individuals responsible for this heinous crime will pay dearly. They belong to an organization known as The Disciples of Forbidden Acts Against Coenobitic Sapotes. Otherwise known as the organization called DFAACS. It would have helped if you had not left out the second "A" in your coded message, but given the fact that you were able to send me a message at all is impressive. No one knows why these people targeted you, but rest assured that your extraction is being coordinated as I type this message. We have analyzed the photographs and have determined a possible location for your extraction point. The people that took you, hereto known as the victims, will pay dearly.
Love,

Pork Chop (aka Carlos)
P.S. Tell them nothing. Remember what we taught you. Smile and drool…

From: Asset Management
Sent: Wednesday, February 13, 2008 10:22 AM
To: Ann; Carlos, Lambie
Cc: All Process Teams
Subject: RE: Running Away
It's a Mission Impossible!!!!

From: Desktop Services
Sent: Wednesday, February 13, 2008 10:54 AM
To: Ann; Carlos, Lambie
Cc: All Process Teams
Subject: RE: Running Away
I recommend we build a database to track all the evidence and movements that may help with this extraction. I will personally start checking all adult sites in case the lil' lamb managed to send a remote clue in one of those videos. It may take me a while, but I am sure I can watch them all. Oh, and look for clues.

From: Security
Sent: Wednesday, February 13, 2008 10:56 AM
To: Ann; Carlos, Lambie
Cc: All Process Teams
Subject: RE: Running Away
Desktop Services,
May I strongly suggest that you do NOT search adult sites for pictures of under-aged lamb….
Security

From: Lambie
Sent: Thursday, February 14, 2008 4:25 PM
To: Ann; Carlos
Cc: All Process Teams
Subject: Re: Running Away

Dear Mommy and Pork Chop,

I'm only able to sneak away for just a moment to send this e-mail because they told me I was not allowed to communicate with the "accused". Fortunately, I was able to use the "back-door" you taught me to get past the pesky security and obtain a rogue PDA. It's been quite a busy couple of days! After being ripped away from our happy cube by DFAACS, I was taken to my foster parents' house. At first, I thought the Fosters were great. Mrs. Foster bought me pajamas and gave me a soft bed to sleep in, and then they gave me my own Barbie to play with. Then, they started saying how I needed to be educated, so they sat me down with a book about counting. Don't they know you've already taught me how to count!? I so miss those times when we counted all the "intellectually challenged" people who sent you e-mails 1, 2, 3, 48, 79, 100. We counted so many in our two short weeks together!

I guess they weren't amused by my wit when I started counting higher than they could, so the next day, they told me if I thought I was so smart, I could just start getting my own food. As you can see in picture 6, Charlie the Fish wasn't much, but it was sure satisfying seeing the look on their faces when they realized he wasn't in his bowl. As you can tell, things are starting to go awry. I'm tired of always being "pressed" to tell them "I love them" and that "they look great". Pork Chop, I think I'm just going to lay low for a while and practice the "Smile and Drool" tactic you taught me to help throw them off!

I hope to be able to write more soon….
Missing you both sooo much,
Lambie

From: Lambie
Sent: Tuesday, March 11, 2008 5:10 PM
To: Carlos; Ann; All Process Teams
Subject: I'm coming home!
Dear Mommy & Pork Chop,
It's been a couple of weeks, but I've finally done it! I'm free!

After being forced to perform cheers while I told them "I loved them" and "they looked great", I vowed it was going to be the last night I ever spent in the Fosters' house! All the fluffiness and wool pajamas are just too much, and I can't take it anymore! When I started counting in binary numbers, they all looked at me like I was dinner. Then, Mommy and Pork Chop, I remembered the first sentence we ever read together:

THERE ARE ONLY 10 TYPES OF PEOPLE IN THE
WORLD—
THOSE WHO UNDERSTAND BINARY, AND THOSE
WHO DON'T.

Before my escape, though, I put the doll in the bed so they will think it is me, safe and asleep. Now, they cannot track me! I did well, huh, Pork Chop?! I thought that would make you proud! Let them try and squeeze Barbie for fawning compliments—ha!

Mommy, not to leave you out, I left them a biting diatribe about the cult-like behaviors of their true organization:

Disciples of Forbidden Acts against Coenobitic Sapotes disguised as the county agency that helps families. Sycophantic idiots!

So, deep in the night, I carefully slid my second-story window open, shimmied down the drain pipe, jumped on the slide, and am heading home! Pork Chop, those tactical maneuvers you taught me are sure coming in handy!

In addition, I've received the transmission you sent and am making my way to the rendezvous point. Please have Chad meet me there. I'll be ready.

I can't wait to see you!

Lambie

From: Lambie
Sent: Tuesday, March 18, 2008 12:17 PM
To: Carlos; Ann; All Process Teams
Subject: Come get me!
Dear Mommy and Pork Chop,
Chad has brought me to the designated pickup point! Per your training, Pork Chop, I've enclosed my location in binary.
Please decode soon and come get me:

01001000000000101101000000100001001001000100010011100
0111000000100101110000001010001000000101
0001000000110101001011001000000000110111101110001100
010110010001010111000011001010000
1001001111011110110100000101010111000100001011001000
0000101000100000101000001010000001000100110100101

I'm so excited!
Love and Hooves,
Lambie

From: Release Management
Sent: Tuesday, March 18, 2008 12:57 PM
To: Lambie; Service Process Improvement
Subject: RE: Come get me!

Lambie,

You forgot to tell us the character encoding you used for your binary message!

I tried ASCII but it gives: H?D!$KZ?,¶AD?-@bEr?A'½ «^Y?^((?4

From: Development
Sent: Tuesday, March 18, 2008 2:36 PM
To: Lambie; All Process Teams
Subject: RE: Come get me!

Lambie,

The number of binary zeros and ones needs to be divisible by 8.

From: Mitchell, Paul
Sent: Tuesday, March 18, 2008 2:53 PM
To: Lambie; All Process Teams
Subject: RE: Come get me!

Lambie,

I know you're excited and your hooves are atwitter to return to your Mom and Porkchop, but you must update your binary location soon or you may become compromised.

Thanks!

Paul

Sadly, that was the last transmission. Lambie was never seen or heard from again. The binary code was supposed to point to a conference room the teams shared where Lambie was waiting underneath the table to be reunited with her mom. When the binary was finally decoded and the extraction team deployed, she was gone. A new search and rescue team was created, but their efforts were fruitless.

If you or someone you know has seen Lambie or knows of her whereabouts, please e-mail Paul or Nicole and let them know. Her family misses her <sniff, sniff>.

[NICOLE'S NOTE: *And if those e-mails from "Pork Chop" or the one from Security to Desktop Services about "under-aged lamb" didn't make your mascara run like a river after a monsoon, your funny bone must have osteoporosis and you need to get to the doctor quick!*]

On a final note, Ann did lighten up...a bit. She starting giving people two strikes instead of one, and if the dark side took hold and she just couldn't contain herself, she would unleash her fury and then quickly come tell Paul about it so he was prepared for it before the customer came screaming. It wasn't much, but we called it progress.

MASCARA ALERT!

Many other occasions over the last few years have required Nicole to dam up the black rivers running down the sides of her face. So, there was this one time…

[NICOLE'S NOTE: …*at band camp?*]
[PAUL'S NOTE: *Really? You're quoting a line from the movie* American Pie *now?*]
[NICOLE'S NOTE: *Well, it was funny, and anytime someone says "This one time…" it makes me think of it.*]
[PAUL'S NOTE: *May I continue on with this mascara alert, please?*]
[NICOLE'S NOTE: *I know which story this is, and I can't believe you're going to share it. It makes you look like such a dumbass.*]
[PAUL'S NOTE: *Did it make your mascara run or not?*]
[NICOLE'S NOTE: *Well, it was 3:00 a.m., so I didn't have much left, but yes, if I had been appropriately made up, I'd have been swimming in a river of black. Carry on.*]

So, there was this one time when Paul and his wife planned a party with their friends to celebrate the opening night of the second installment of one very huge sparkling vampire movie series. Everyone had waited anxiously for months for this movie to come out and, after the midnight premier of the movie, a small group of people from the party decided to go the local twenty-four-hour pancake house to continue to rave about the movie was and dissect every scene.

Paul, Nicole, Ann (from the Lambie story), Marie (the first member in the Hooves High club), Alyssa (Nicole's mulatta friend, whom she had dubbed her HAN--hot ass niece--even though they're not related), and Kenny (Nicole's son) all rushed into the restaurant, laughing and talking about the movie.

"Six for breakfast, please," Paul called out to the one lonely waitress manning the whole place.

"Booth or table?" she asked, obviously assaulted by the cheeriness of the crowd at three o'clock in the morning.

"Table, please," Paul responded.

"I want a booth," Nicole challenged.

"Me, too," Alyssa chimed in, fully supporting her HAA (hot ass aunt).

"Really?" Paul rolled his eyes.

"How about both?" the waitress offered.

"Perfect," they all sung in unison.

After returning with everyone's drinks, the waitress was ready to take orders. Ann went first, substituting and changing everything possible. The waitress remained calm, answering her questions and dutifully making all the required alterations.

Next, Marie was up. She ordered some sort of sausage concoction rolled in a pancake. She wanted it topped with fresh strawberries but the waitress had to think about that and then go check on it.

[PAUL'S NOTE: *Being a true Hoofer, we appreciate Marie's dedication to the perfect breakfast food. Hooves High, Marie! Hooves High!*]

When the waitress returned, confirming Marie's fruit selection, she turned to Paul. "And what would you like?"

"Three eggs and pancakes, please," he replied, casting a disapproving look over at Ann and Marie for not being able to just order straight from the menu without making substitutions.

"Do you want real eggs?" Nicole interjected.

"What do you mean, 'Do I want real eggs?'" Paul mimicked. "I just said I wanted three *eggs* and pancakes."

"You know you have to request real eggs here."

"What are you talking about?"

"They use powdered eggs."

With that, Paul turned around and looked at the waitress, hoping she would let him in on the joke. Nothing. He looked at Nicole.

"Eggs here are made from powder?" Paul questioned.

"Yes, they just add a little water and bring them back to life," Nicole continued.

Unable to imagine such a thing, Paul turned back around to the waitress and demanded a response. "Is this true?"

"Well, uh," she stammered, "we do use powdered eggs here, but you can request shelled eggs."

"Are you kidding me?" Paul shot back, utterly repulsed. "You listen here. I want my eggs shelled and fresh from the anus. I don't want any of this powdered mess."

"You want them what?" the waitress asked, taking a slight step back in case Paul was turning crazy and she needed to run for the panic button.

"I want my eggs fresh from the anus. Three of them. Scrambled, with cheese. Your cheese isn't powdered, is it?"

"No, sir."

"Thank God."

By this time, Ann had her head buried deep in her lap out of mortification, HAN was sitting next to Nicole with her mouth open, and Kenny was laughing like a hyena and shaking the whole table.

The waitress quickly took the rest of the table's order and retreated. She only returned one more time to deliver the food and the check at the same time, and that was it. She had had enough.

"You know what?" Paul said, after taking a few bites of his fresh-from-the-anus eggs. "Now that I know about the powdered eggs here, this whole place looks dirtier to me. Like I'm just now noticing how dirty the window shades are. And look at those seats over there. They have a tear in them. This whole place is just subpar." He cast a few more disapproving glances at his surroundings and then pushed his plate away. Even Hoofers have standards.

The next week at work, Paul grabbed Nicole and told her they had an important task to get done. Nicole got up, not knowing what Paul was talking about, and followed him down the hall and into the cafeteria. Approaching the cafeteria manager, Paul said, "Tony, I need to know something, and it's important."

"Okay," Tony said, looking up at them like they'd just found a hair in his food.

"Are your eggs from the anus?" Paul asked.

"Are they what?" Tony bellowed, holding up his spatula-like knife.

"You know, do you shell your eggs every morning or do you make them from powder?" Paul replied testily while keeping an eyeball on the spatula.

"Oh," Tony nodded, now understanding the question and lowering his weapon. "No, we shell all our eggs daily. We'd never offer you powdered eggs."

"Whew. I just found out about powdered eggs at our local pancake house, and I've been in a state of shock ever since. It's been most upsetting."

"Well, nothing to worry about here. Ours are indeed from the anus."

"Great! We'll see you later, Tony. Pot pie, right?"

"Yep."

"That's our favorite. See ya."

[PAUL'S NOTE: *As we've recounted this story, many people have questioned whether or not eggs really do come from a chicken's anus. The short answer is yes. Chickens only have one hole, called a "vent", that everything comes out of. They also don't have urine. They have a white pasty substance called "urates". Bet you're sorry you even wondered now, aren't you? LOL.*]

Trimming The Fat

Your team's strength is measured not only by the amount of work its members do, but also by the amount of fun they have while doing it. Team-building activities are a way to do just that. If you can do it in a manner that gets everyone involved and is fun, you'll build a team and strengthen bonds without them even knowing it (just like that freshman fifteen).

LMAOPIMP

Meaning
Laughing my ass off peeing in my pants.

Heart of the Story
Nicole is the only one with incontinence problems around here, so she gets credit for this one.

Everyone knows what LOL means. You've read something that's funny and it made you giggle, usually out loud. Sometimes you read something that really makes you laugh, and then you're LMAO, or 'laughing my ass off'. If you get to the point where you're laughing so hard you know if you don't stop you're going to leave a wet spot in your seat, then you're LMAOPIMP, or 'laughing my ass off peeing in your pants'.

Unlike LOL and LMAO, though, LMAOPIMP lasts for more than a few seconds. When something is so funny that you are LMAOPIMPing, it's usually something that even after you've re-gained a small ounce of control, if you start thinking about it again, you're back on another LMAOPIMP ride and you're bringing oth-ers on the trip with you!

When you are LMAOPIMPing, it will typically cause those around you to LOL, even when they have no clue as to why they're LOLing. Yes, LMAOPIMP is contagious. It's the true swine flu and, no, we don't mean the H1N1 flu. No, this is the swine flu in its intended form, the kind that makes the "other white meat" wholesalers happy. It's the snorting you spout when you hear something so funny that your true laugh comes out instead of your ersatz office laugh. It's the laugh that becomes so infectious that everyone around you starts giggling, unsure of the joke, yet unable to help themselves from joining in on the laughter. It's the kind of funny that causes you pain. It's more than ROFL (rolling on the floor laughing); it's PIMPing!

Paul and Nicole have shared a few of these moments over the years, and every time they think about them, uncontrollable snorting ensues. Two of those stories follow.

Tail

Okay, seriously, we have never laughed so hard in our lives. We're talking full-on, on-the-floor hot flashes. Unfortunately, this series of hot flashes was at the expense of none other than our good friend, Tina, and how she changed from the Good Witch of the East to the Wicked Witch of the West before our very eyes (bless her heart).

[NICOLE'S NOTE: *First, let me stop you right here if you think I am old enough for hot flashes. I am not, and may the Curse of a Thousand Doughnuts befall you if you thought I was. These hot flashes are totally different. These occur not from old age, but from laughing so hard that sound ceases to come from your mouth, your cheekbones start to hurt, and you get all hot and flustered, just like a hot flash (or so I've heard).*]

We've already told you how we like to have tea in the afternoons. Well, some afternoons in the spring, right before the heat from the sun becomes too unbearable and hateful, we skip tea and go outside for a brisk, fifteen-minute walk around our building instead. It was on one of those fateful days when Tina did the unthinkable... in public.

It started off like any other spring afternoon in April. Nicole and Paul were debating whether or not they wanted to go to the cafeteria for tea or go outside and walk. The thought of Key lime cheesecake was weighing heavily on their minds (for they hadn't had it in over a week and were suffering from withdrawal), and they knew a vigorous fifteen-minute jaunt around the building would be all they'd need to negate any calorie accumulation from the cheesecake should the opportunity to get some arise later.

[PAUL'S NOTE: *You know about the special rules of calorie accumulation, right? For instance, calories don't count if you simply eat dessert from the dish it comes in. The same goes for those scoops of dough you test before you make the cookies or that batter you lick and put nose prints in after you pour it in the pan to bake. Yes, just like dancing to a song with your kids in the living room or taking a brief walk around the building at work, calories won't count or stick if you do some quick exercising right before you indulge. Promise.*]

Deciding the forecast for Key lime cheesecake was looking good that day, just like the weather outside, they called Tina to see if she could join them. Thrilled to spend time with two of her favorite subjects, Tina bopped right over. Dressed in a black pantsuit with black high heels, she looked quite queenly that day.

[NICOLE'S NOTE: *I believe she even did the beauty pageant wave as she walked over. So dramatic she is.*]

"So, which path are we taking today?" Tina asked. "The one near the break area, or the one near the road?"

"Um, let's take the one near the break area," Paul said. "We can pass by the koi pond and see how the fish are doing."

So they set off, picking up their pace once they got outside. Nicole likes to keep her arms at ninety degrees and move them back and forth vigorously when she walks like she's a professional walker. She's sure it helps burn even more calories.

[PAUL'S NOTE: *Whatever. You look like you're cross-country skiing. It's stupid.*]
[NICOLE'S NOTE: *You're just jealous you're not burning more calories than me and that I'll be in my skinny jeans quicker. Get over it.*]

The koi pond was the first stop on their trek, and they crossed over the tiny wooden bridge and looked down at the fish, enjoying its interesting placement in the middle of a break area at a manufacturing plant. As they continued, the conversation turned to different weight-loss techniques.

"You know," Nicole started, "I'm really thinking about doing a colonic. Everything I've read says they're really effective."

"You want an anal cleanse?" Paul retorted, stopping in midstride. Tina halted, too, and burst into laughter.

Turning to see Paul and Tina motionless, Nicole walked back. "I do not want an 'anal cleanse'. I want a colonic," Nicole said wryly.

"No, you do. You either want to take a pill that's going to cause your intestines to push the shit out, or you want to stick a hose up your ass to wash the shit out. Which is it?"

"Umm," Nicole stammered, "I was thinking about the pill, but I was hoping for something a little gentler. There are different types of colonics. I want the one that addresses yeastiness."

"What?" Tina jumped in. "Are you having problems 'down there'?" she asked, pointing to her nether regions.

"No! Of course not!" Nicole fired back. "Mama keeps her pipes clean! This is to address yeastiness within your whole body. You know I'm a carbohydrate whore. I think it will be perfect."

"Perfectly stupid," Paul quipped. "We both know the only thing that will purge you of yeastiness is giving up bread, including those yeast rolls you love so much! You and your poop purge have fun. Can we please change the subject?"

"Yes, please," Tina pleaded, and she began walking again.

They rounded the back part of the building, where some construction was going on. Most of the construction workers were on break and sitting on the back of their pickup trucks, munching on snacks or drinking water. As they passed each one, Nicole and Tina had to speak, each convinced their handout of sunshine and smiles was the best.

"Hey there! How are you today?" Nicole called out, grinning and waving at everyone.

"It looks like you guys have been working hard! It looks great!" Tina shouted, just an octave higher than Nicole and waving just a little more rapidly. As Tina did this, she glanced over at Nicole, running her eyes up and down, ensuring that Nicole understood she was the queen.

Satisfied with their performance, they made their way through the parking lot, avoiding the buildup of mud that had accumulated in some spots from the construction equipment. As they made it to the other side, the sidewalk became available again, and they hopped back on, Paul in tow.

Then, while passing the last group of construction workers on the sidewalk, it happened.

In public.

The unthinkable.

Tina fell.

She was blabbing on about how nice everyone was and how good the new construction looked, and then, all of a sudden, she stopped talking and began wobbling. Almost as if in a cartoon or in slow motion, she wobbled back and forth on her two-inch heels for a long, long moment.

Then, as a sign she had finally given in, her neck went limp.

Followed by her torso.

Finally, she fell to the side and melted to the ground.

There was a long moment of silence before anyone spoke. It was like watching a train wreck: painful to watch, but you just couldn't look away. Paul and Nicole stood there frozen, unsure if they should scream or offer a hand. The construction workers were equally aghast, just sitting there motionless. And there was Tina. Floundering on the dirty sidewalk like a fish without water, jerking and gasping.

"Tina, are you okay?" Paul finally asked.

"Oh my God, Tina!" Nicole shrieked, and they both ran to her side.

"I-I-I, um, yeah, I think so," Tina stammered. She sat up, looking quite stunned.

"Let me help you up," Paul offered, and extended his hand. Tina took it, and Paul felt the gravel still clinging to her palm.

Once erect, Tina looked around, blinking from the brightness of the sun. Nicole picked up Tina's once fashionable Jackie O sunglasses, now marred by the bitter concrete, and handed them to her. "Thank you, Nicole," she said, proudly placing them back on. She then commenced to brush the dirt and debris from her pantsuit. Surprisingly, her shoes remained intact.

"Are you okay?" Paul asked again.

"Yeah, I just can't believe I did a gravity check in public! Look at me. I'm a mess, and I can tell there are going to be bruises everywhere tomorrow. Let's just keep moving."

"Are you sure?" Nicole pressed.

"Yes, yes, I'm really fine," Tina assured her. "Let's roll, people."

"Tina, one more time, you're sure you're okay?" Paul pushed.

"Yes! Nothing is bruised here but my ego. Can we move? Everyone is staring!" And with that, Paul let out a laugh so loud, the buildings shook.

"Oh my God, Tina, I'm so glad you're okay because that was the funniest thing I have ever seen in my life!" He wrapped his arms around his stomach, clenched them tight, and continued laughing hysterically.

"Really?" Tina hissed. "You have to do this here?"

"I (gasp) can't (gasp) help (gasp) it!" Paul pleaded with her. "You don't do (gasp) anything normal (gasp), do you?"

"What do you mean?" Tina said, clearly offended now.

"Did you see how you fell (gasp)?" Paul tried to slow his convulsions to recount the story. "You didn't just fall over like a normal person. No, you rocked back and forth on your heels forever (gasp), and then, when you did decide to fall, you had 'gay neck'!" More fits of laughter.

"What is *gay neck*?" Tina and Nicole demanded together.

"Hang on, give me a second here." Paul breathed heavily. After a minute or so, he continued, "Have you never seen Carlos Mencia's *Performance Enhanced* DVD? Oh my God, oh my God, *oh my God!* In this one bit, he describes how when he was over in Iraq performing for the troops, some mortars dropped and began exploding. He knew that when you heard mortars exploding, you were supposed to hit the deck. He'd practiced falling 'like a man,' but when the time came, he had 'gay neck.' Basically he fell forward, neck first, followed by his body going limp, and went into a final, weak descent to the ground. He imitated it on stage, and it was exactly what you did. It was hilarious! Friggin' hilarious!"

[PAUL'S NOTE: *Please, please note, this is not intended, in any way whatsoever, to offend anyone who is gay or lesbian. Nicole and I have many,*

many gay and lesbian friends, and we love you all. If you haven't seen Carlos Mencia's DVD either, please don't take offense at his joke. You have to see the whole bit to appreciate it. All our gays love it, so go buy or rent a copy today. You'll be LMAOPIMPing.]

At this point, Paul imitated gay neck…in public…demonstrating every movement, even mock falling to the ground. Seeing the reenactment, Nicole burst into hysterics. "Tina, he's right! It really was like that!"

"Really? I had gay neck?" Tina asked, somewhat amused.

"*Yes!*" Paul laughed, relieved that she was starting to see the humor in the situation. All the way back to the office, as Tina began to limp slightly, Paul imitated gay neck for them, driving Nicole further and further into fits of laughter.

Once back inside, Paul and Nicole dragged Tina around to every office and cube recounting the story, each time adding little tidbits to make the story more audacious than it already was.

Realizing this was a great way for her to get even more attention from her subjects, Tina began playing along, adding in her own flare here and there. At one point, toward the end, she even starting playing up the part of gay neck, mimicking her own fall and laughing just as hard as the audience did. For a good hour, the three of them paraded around laughing and having a good time, all at Tina's expense.

She was a great sport, and even though she came in with a severely bruised leg the next day, the fun continued. Paul brought in his copy of Carlos's *Performance Enhanced* DVD and played the gay neck part for them. That started a whole new round of hysteria and even more retellings of the story from the day before.

At the end of their fun-filled week, the three of them used their Friday afternoon tea to recap.

[PAUL'S NOTE: *Yes, we have afternoon tea—you British people don't get to hog this tradition. And, with Tina still limping, we were relegated to tea every day for a while.*]

"Tina, I have to tell you, I don't know when I have ever laughed so hard," Nicole started. "I was so worried you were really hurt, and then we found out you weren't, and Paul started imitating you, I thought I was going to die. I just about peed my pants on the walk back here that day!"

"I know!" Tina said, laughing. "I still can't believe I fell in public like that. Who does that? Who falls as an adult? I'm still a little mortified."

"You should be," Paul scoffed. "You fell on the smallest, most microscopic pebble in the entire parking lot. You dodged all the big rocks construction dug up, but you managed to wobble for five minutes on a teeny, tiny one. It was like watching a cartoon character fall the way you stayed on it and balanced so long. Hysterical! I have told that story to everyone, and it never gets old. Why do we laugh at other people's misfortunes? Why is that funny?"

"Who cares? It just is," Tina said.

"Okay, so Tina, you know how when you let us in on the secret of Mondo! And we told you it was like you were the Good Witch of the East bestowing a new power on us?" Nicole asked.

"Yeah," Tina replied, cautiously.

"Well, when you fell, you turned into the Wicked Witch of the West, because watching that was like watching you melt. *Heeelllppp meeeeee!*" Nicole mimicked the witch, with her hands up in the air in mock agony.

Fits of laughter from the whole table.

"Stop! I can't take any more this week! My cheeks still hurt," Paul gasped, trying to regain control.

"Well, I predict we won't have another set of laughs like this for a while," Nicole said, channeling her inner Oracle.

"Good!" Tina said. "You don't see me falling again anytime soon, do you?"

"No, sweetie, I think you've met your lifetime quota."

Strap on your Depends for this One

If you've ever worked in a professional environment, then the word "re-org" is probably a familiar term. Usually a couple of times a year, people get moved around under different managers or directors to try to better align with the company's current direction. Rumors of re-orgs begin circulating weeks before they actually happen, and tensions run high. Phishers run around turning tiny bits of information they've heard into large tales of job loss, massive restructuring, and huge upsets in power.

[NICOLE'S NOTE: *We'll get to the chapter on phishers soon and my tail about Santa's thong. Mmnt! For now, suffice it to say that these are the gossip whores. If you want to get the real scoop, you must befriend a resource hog.*]

After one such re-org, Paul and Nicole found themselves among new faces, and their executive director wanted all the managers to gather together, introduce themselves, and talk about the plans for their teams over the next twelve months.

Because Hoofers stick together like a herd, Paul and Nicole found two seats side by side and waited. Paul was called on first to introduce himself, which he did, proudly listing the accomplishments his teams had achieved and passing out an organized list of objectives for the upcoming year.

[NICOLE'S NOTE: *Always the show-off having to one-up everyone else. We weren't even supposed to bring anything. The point of the meeting was to brainstorm objectives.*]

[PAUL'S NOTE: *I know, but I just wanted to intimidate everyone else who was new to the team (and give them disapproving sideways glances when they said they hadn't thought that far ahead). Mmnt!*]

For some reason, the introductions continued with everyone to Paul's right, and since Nicole was on his left, that meant she would go last.

[NICOLE'S NOTE: *Always saving the best for last, baby!*]

[PAUL'S NOTE: *Except that day! LMAOPIMP!*]

Finally, it was Nicole's turn. She stood up, arched her back, sucked it in, batted her eyelashes, and smiled her best sunshiny smile. "Hello, everyone! My name is Nicole, and I am so happy we are all on the same team…"

"Umm, Nicole?" Paul interrupted.

Nicole glanced down at Paul and gave him the "WTF are you doing?" look.

"Is your shirt on backward?" Paul asked, amplifying his voice, with his eyes growing bigger with each word.

"What?" Nicole screeched, looking down at her shirt.

"Oh my God! It is!" Paul screeched back.

Looking around at her executive director and the other managers in the room, who were now solely focused on the seams of her shirt, Nicole was stunned and speechless.

[PAUL'S NOTE: *Which was the first and last time I have ever seen her that way.*]

Huge outbursts of laughter erupted. Everyone was pointing and cracking up.

[NICOLE'S NOTE: *Yes, they were all laughing at me. It was horrible!*]

[PAUL'S NOTE: *Correction. They were laughing* with *you.*]
[NICOLE'S NOTE: *Did you see me laughing? Mmnt!*]

Unsure what to do next, Nicole finally said, "Umm, excuse me for just a moment, everyone, while I go put myself back together."

"Yes, make sure it's the correct way this time," Paul called after her, tears streaming down his face.

[NICOLE'S NOTE: *Hateful!*]
[PAUL'S NOTE: *Let's be honest. We knew everyone in that room. We'd just never been on the same team with them before. It was hilarious, and it was a great tension breaker.*]
[NICOLE'S NOTE: *At my expense! I should sue you for mental anguish!*]
[PAUL'S NOTE: *Then I will sue you for unexpected loss of bladder control. I think I dribbled some in my pants because I was laughing so hard!*]

Returning to the room just a minute later, hair a little out of place, Nicole gave the whole room a long glance, smiled, and said, "I'm back and all together now. And, thank you, Paul, for pointing out my fashion faux pas in front of *everyone*. I only wish you could have told me *before* I'd stood and began speaking." Death stare and daggers.

[PAUL'S NOTE: *I do regret blurting it out like that, but it was honestly the first time I noticed it. It was just unfortunate how you were already standing up and speaking in front of all our new teammates when I did. Bwhahaahaaa <tears>. Oh, wait, I need a* bathroom now...]
[NICOLE'S NOTE: *And you were on my defecation roster for weeks after that!*]
[PAUL'S NOTE: *What's a defecation roster?*]
[NICOLE'S NOTE: *My shit list.*]

[PAUL'S NOTE: *Ohhhh, LOL. Sorry, Nic.*]

◆ ◆ ◆

Trimming the Fat

Not only can laughter build relationships within your team, it can build new relationships outside your team as well. Finding the funny in any situation and using it as a way to break the ice will create good will and open you up to new conversations that could turn into long-lasting relationships (just like the one with your favorite dessert).

Eight Pounds, Six Ounces

Meaning

When something heavenly happens and praises need to be sung, throw your spirit fingers in the air and praise little eight-pound, six-ounce Baby Jesus (or any other baby deity of your choosing).

Heart of the Story

We can't take credit for coining this phrase, but we can certainly take credit for glorifying it.

In the movie *Talladega Nights*, Will Ferrell's character, Ricky Bobby, is at the dinner table, saying grace to none other than Baby Jesus. Ricky's grace is interrupted as a discussion ensues as to who is the proper Jesus to pray to: Baby Jesus, adult Jesus, or even rocker Jesus (courtesy of his friend, Cal). Eventually, Ricky regains control of the prayer and makes it known that the person who brings in the millions is the one who prays, and he can therefore pray to whichever Jesus he likes, and he prefers praying to the Baby Jesus in the manger.

[NICOLE'S NOTE: *"Dear eight-pound six-ounce Baby Jesus, newborn, not even spoken a word yet."* OMG! That whole scene was the funniest thing I have ever heard! The writers of Talladega Nights *truly are amazing with MAD SKILLZ! Word!*]

[PAUL'S NOTE: *For those of you not familiar with Ebonics, allow me to provide a translation. "Mad skillz" means they are talented. "Word," as Nicole uses it here, is like saying "for real."*]

[NICOLE'S NOTE: *Who are you, the old lady from* Airplane? *"Oh, stewardess! I speak jive." I'm sure they all know what "mad skillz" and "word" mean.*]

[PAUL'S NOTE: *Whatever!*]

What made that scene even funnier for Nicole was that her son, Kenny, was also eight pounds, six ounces when he was born, so she couldn't help but be hooked on the saying.

[PAUL'S NOTE: *And she's spent every waking moment since then hooking everyone else, including me.*]

"Eight pounds, six ounces" took off, and every time Nicole used it in the company of those who weren't familiar with it, she'd initially receive a giggle only to be followed up with those persons shouting the tag line and waving their hands for their own praises later on.

Tail

It was just one of those days. Nicole had been avoiding calls from an overly ambitious software vendor who wanted to come in and audit the number of times their software had been installed on employees' computers. Nicole is not one to normally duck and dive because her asset management tool could have easily provided her with that information and gotten the pushy vendor off her back. The problem was Robert, the guy she'd inherited to manage the tool.

Robert was young, energetic, and passionate. The issue was he didn't want to do simple tasks, such as pulling a report. Instead, he wanted to focus on implementing every new bell and whistle the tool offered. He would give his best sales pitch to the IT gods to try to get funding and support for his every whim. Nine times out of ten, though, he fumbled the football before he was anywhere near the end zone, and he usually walked away pretty beat up and bruised from the sack.

The most unfortunate part about all this is that like Hans and Franz from *Saturday Night Live*, Robert didn't have the brains to back up his overly inflated ego.

[PAUL & NICOLE'S NOTE: *We want to pump <clap> YOU UP!*]

He used a consultant named Anthony to learn about the new bells and whistles, but whenever Anthony tried to share his pearls of wisdom, Robert ignored them. The result was that Robert would implement the enhancements directly in production and cause outages and, consequently, create distrust in the application from the IT gods.

Something had to be done. The software vendor was turning up the heat to perform the audit, and Nicole was trying to find the fire extinguisher to put out that flame! What was the hot asset manager to do?

[PAUL'S NOTE: *Why are we referring to you as the "hot" asset manager?*]
[NICOLE'S NOTE: *Because I am. No more interruptions.*]

Fortunately for Nicole, Robert was getting married and he and his fiancée were moving out of state to be closer to family. So once he put in his three-week notice, Nicole did the happy dance. Oh yes, she had *high hopes*, just like that little ant in the Frank Sinatra song who was trying to move the rubber tree. High hopes that she was going to find an amazing administrator, one who could do the work he was asked to do and could speak humbly, yet intelligently, to the IT gods. Yes, Nicole was on the hunt, like the lioness she is.

[PAUL'S NOTE: *Wait. First you're hot, and now you're a lioness?*]
[NICOLE'S NOTE: *I'm not sure what the problem is. It's like I'm sensing something. Hmmm, could that be a tinge of Hater-Ade?*]
[PAUL'S NOTE: *Really? Hater-Ade? Can we just get on with the story?*]
[NICOLE'S NOTE: *Hater!*]

Nicole assumed the hiring process was going to be easy peasy, one, two, threesy. *Wrong!*

The résumés poured in, one after another. Things looked promising until Nicole noticed an unfortunate trend. None of the candidates appeared to have any experience. It was like Robert was applying—tens of Roberts! Even so, Nicole, with her usual sunshine, glass-half-full outlook, began to schedule interviews, hoping for the best.

Her first interview was with Peter. Peter was, to say the least, a total letdown.

[PAUL'S NOTE: *Kinda like when you get to the bottom of a bowl of ice cream and you know there's no more in the freezer to fill it back up with <sigh>.*]

Not only did Peter seem to forget he had a phone interview, he sounded as if Nicole had woken him up when she called him. He had to think about every answer, including the typical question, "So how long have you been in IT?" It was obvious at the end of her phone interview that Peter was *not* getting a call back.

Pam was more interesting. She had a great personality over the phone. She was bright and bubbly, and, right off the bat, she spoke as if she were already a member of the team. She was fairly knowledgeable about how to use the tool, but when asked more technical questions, she seemed to stutter a bit. Still, Nicole thought Pam had been the best phone interview thus far and requested an in-person interview.

Nicole's in-person interviews were very different from her phone interviews. She asked a few technical questions that were direct and to the point. If you couldn't answer those properly, like in *American Idol*, you were not invited to Hollywood. If you made it past that, she continued with questions like, "If you could get rid of any state in the country, which state would you get rid of and why?" She wanted to see how the person would act when caught off guard. Often, when Robert was caught off guard by the IT gods, his natural response was defensive posturing that led down the wrong path and ended up with Nicole stroking a lot of godly egos. And you know how that goes. If you stroke one god, you've got to stroke them all.

[NICOLE'S NOTE: *<sigh> A good manager's job is never easy and never done!*]
[PAUL'S NOTE: *Whatever! You ended up with those guys eating out of the palm of your hand. They loved you, and you loved every minute of it!*]
[NICOLE'S NOTE: *Shhh. They might be reading. Stop interrupting the story or we'll never get done. Interrupting whore!*]

On the day of Pam's in-person interview, Nicole was beaming. She just knew Pam was a kindred spirit and had boasted and bragged to Paul that he would love her. She had already pictured Pam as a member of the party-planning committee and had imagined the creative foods she would bring to the potlucks. Yes, Nicole liked Pam and had already made up her mind to hire her if the interview went well.

Paul had been busy that morning and hadn't had a moment to see Nicole before the interview.

"Why are you so dressed up?" Paul inquired with distress in his voice. "Do you have an interview? You know you can't leave me! Mmnt!"

Nicole responded in her most "you dumb ass" of voices. "No, silly, we're interviewing Pam. Remember?"

"Oh shoot. That's right. I completely forgot. Wait. Then why are you dressed up? Did you dress up for *Pam?*"

"Well, yes," Nicole answered, now feeling like the kid at the playground who was just caught eating the store-brand Oreos and not the real ones. "I just wanted her to see our professionalism and class. That's all," she continued, trying to rebound from the sting of humiliation before it actually set in and ruined her spirit.

"Okay, let's go see who you're drooling over," Paul teased.

Nicole, eager to meet Pam, flung open the conference room with just a bit more zest than even she expected, and there, standing in the corner, was Pam, a tall, scraggly woman. She had wiry, layered blond hair that confused Paul and Nicole. It had the characteristics of being somewhat feathered on the sides, but it was short on top and long in the back, like a feathered mullet. To make matters worse, it was untamed, like a small animal had taken hold of her head and wouldn't let go. The lioness in Nicole was roaring loudly, and she was trying hard to resist the urge to pounce. Paul, whose hair is always immaculate and never with a strand out of place, seemed almost in pain as he looked at it.

As if the feathery, animal-like mullet on her head wasn't bad enough, they were accosted by her outfit. It also was confusing. The black top looked like something she must have worn the previous night at the club. The spaghetti straps held up a low, v-cut front that exposed the cavernous gap between her almost nonexistent girls. The worst part, if there is such a thing after witnessing the train wreck she called her hair, was that the top didn't completely cover her stomach when she moved. As she walked over to greet them, her belly button and accompanying belly button ring exposed themselves. Needless to say, that was not at all something Nicole, in all her hotness, would wear (or expose).

[PAUL'S NOTE: *We were going so well. I let the "lioness" comment go. But really? In all your hotness?*]

[NICOLE'S NOTE: *I think you're still thirsty. That Hater-Ade you're drinking must be a bit* salty, *just like your cookies.*]

Wondering if Pam had chosen to put the black top back on this morning after wearing it to the club last night or if she still hadn't taken it off, Nicole moved on to the lower half of the outfit. She noticed her black jeans didn't seem to fit her quite right. Something was wrong, and then it dawned on her. They were men's jeans. The hairstyle wasn't really feminine, but it wasn't really masculine either. The top was definitely feminine, but now the pants were very masculine. What was going on?

Then there were Pam's feet, or rather what she had on them. She wore thick, white, men's socks with tennis shoes that had definitely been around the block more than a few times. Yes, Pam's outfit flashed like a yellow light at a dangerous intersection. *Danger! Danger! Danger!*

The interview was a blur. Rather than interviewing her separately, Paul simply stayed and listened in on Nicole's interview, only chiming in occasionally to repeat some crazy comment Pam would make, like how she might be late sometimes because she had a tendency to sleep in.

[PAUL & NICOLE'S NOTE: *Even if you are the type who likes to hit the snooze button fifteen times, and this situation really could happen to you, never mention it in an interview, okay?*]

They couldn't get out of there fast enough. Pam seemed so different from what either of them expected, and when they received the information from her background check, they knew why.

[NICOLE'S NOTE: *Brace yourselves.*]

[PAUL'S NOTE: *Seriously, grab something sturdy before you read the next line.*]

Pam had been convicted on two prior counts of prostitution. Really.

"Oh my God!" Nicole screamed. "She's a ho!"

"Well, that explains the outfit, I guess, and why she said she likes to sleep in. But who would pay money for that?" Paul asked. "Seriously, she'd have to get me really drunk and then pay me before I ever went fishing in that hole."

"Maybe there are guys out there who like the ridden-hard-and-put-up-wet look," Nicole guessed.

"Well, you thought she sounded *great* on the phone, and you even dressed up for her. Is there something I need to know about you?" Paul teased.

"Mmnt. Well, we've still got a phone interview with Jonathan coming up. He's out of state, so maybe we'll have some luck there."

[PAUL'S NOTE: *Not.*]

Jonathan had been in IT for almost twenty years and had the experience they were looking for. Nicole and Paul teamed up for the phone interview.

Without fail, though, just like the other two candidates, Jonathan quickly went from *why not* to just *why*. Every technical question asked was either a textbook answer or "I've got a friend who can help with that."

"We need a lot of different types of reports created. Are you familiar with SQL queries?" Paul probed.

"Well, I'm not, but I have a coworker that works behind me who's a SQL whiz. I can just ask him for help," Jonathan responded. Immediately, Paul looked at Nicole, and they both had the same thought. *How the hell is he going to ask his coworker about* our *SQL database? He isn't even going to be at the same company anymore!*

"Hmm, how would you work with him on it?" Nicole inquired, very interested in how Jonathan was going to convince her that this would be successful.

"Well, it would have to be after hours, of course, but I'd just grant him access to the server," he answered very matter-of-factly, as if Nicole had insulted him for some reason.

"And how would you do that?" Nicole continued, unaffected by his tone.

"I'd give him my ID and password so he could log in, of course," Jonathan replied in his most "dumb ass" of tones.

Now, if it was one thing Nicole did not appreciate, it was being called a dumb ass, and that's exactly what his tone suggested. Paul, realizing that the lioness was about to attack, quickly threw his arm out, restraining her from getting any closer to the phone, and swiftly asked another question.

"Okaaay, so your résumé suggests you have network and server administration experience. Are you comfortable setting up a new server and adding asset management software to it for our development environment?"

"Well, I've never really set up a fresh server before," Jonathan replied.

"Uh-huh," Nicole interrupted.

"But I have a friend...."

"Of course you do," Nicole interrupted again, which brought a swift nudge from Paul to get her back on her best behavior.

"I'm sure he can walk me through the process," Jonathan responded with irritation in his voice.

"Let me ask you something," Nicole began, mimicking his irritation and adding a neck roll that was not only visible to Paul but that was conveyed over the phone in her tone as well. "Your résumé says you've supported my asset management tool for a year and have a network and server background. How have you supported it, and what have you done?"

"Well," Jonathan began with a bit of hesitation, recognizing that the lioness was intimidating now and that he should proceed with caution, "I've been working on our Help Desk for a year now, and we use the same asset management tool. So sometimes we have issues with it, and our administrator will let me watch while he works on it."

"*Watch?* So you've never actually supported it on your own?" Nicole emphasized. Score one for Nicole.

"Well, no, but I am certified," Jonathan offered, trying to rebound from his loss of that round.

"Uh-huh. And how long have you been certified?"

Jonathan responded, very proudly, "Four months."

Nicole simply looked at Paul and mouthed, "Robert."

At that moment, Jonathan decided it was time for him to begin the questioning. "I have a few questions as well."

"Shoot," Paul responded in his most upbeat of voices, trying to recharge the energy of the conversation.

"Benefits are very important to me and my family," and he began a line of questions related to medical, dental, and 401(k) benefits. Paul and Nicole were simply stunned, but the worst was yet to come.

"Well, you seem like a company I could work for."

"Is that right?" Nicole responded, unamused. She had her finger on the trigger, ready to hit the speaker button to hang up on his crazy ass just as soon as she could.

"Let's talk salary. I'm expecting, based on the responsibilities, that I'll be somewhere in the six-figure range," Jonathan suggested.

"Is that so?" Nicole chuckled out her response.

"Yes, I understand my experience is probably not as long as a more senior technician."

[NICOLE'S NOTE: *This was probably the first and only statement made by this guy the entire interview that I agreed with.*]

"So, I understand I won't be offered a salary in the mid one hundreds; however, I think you should know that I cannot accept anything under one hundred even," Jonathan finished. The tone of his voice was that of the winning boxer talking with the reporter at the end of the fight. He had been banged up and bruised but never completely out for the count. He had won, and he was ready to reap his rewards.

And with that comment, Nicole attacked. Running the fifty-four fake out to maneuver from around Paul's wingspan, Nicole went in for the kill. Hard!

"Jonathan. First let me say that it has been a true pleasure interviewing you. Never before in all my interviews have I encountered someone such as yourself."

"Why thank you," Jonathan interjected.

"No," Nicole continued, "I think you misunderstand. I have never interviewed someone who has so blatantly misrepresented himself. It's like we were meeting for the first time after online dating, and you've sent a picture of Tom Cruise when you're really Billy Bob. To have the audacity to ask for a six-figure income with no experience is absolutely the most absurd, yet funniest thing I've heard in quite some time. Yes, Jonathan, I would like to thank you for providing me with the story of the day. I'm sure, in time, Paul and I will look back on these last forty-five minutes as office entertainment versus what we are each thinking now…a waste of time where we could have been doing something more productive than this.

"However, I do feel it's my responsibility to grow you into a better interviewee. After all, that's what a good manager would do, and I am very good at my job. So let me leave you with this. Several times, your tone was patronizing and disparaging. That's not something I would suggest you do on your next interview. You should change your résumé to fit the experience you *actually* have and not what your family, friends or coworkers have. I would also suggest you apply for jobs on your experience level, such as *junior* admin positions.

And last, *never, never* discuss salary within the first interview. Very unprofessional.

"I've learned a valuable lesson to just go with my instincts. I should have cut you short earlier in the interview instead of thinking I would just take what was given to me. Thank you, Jonathan, thank you. And no, you will not be getting a call back or the job. Good day!"

And with that, like a scorpion sting, Nicole hit the speaker button and hung up on Jonathan without waiting for his response. Game, set, match.

Paul, shocked and amazed, wasn't quite sure what to say. On one hand, he totally agreed with Nicole and felt someone needed to school Jonathan. On the other hand, he was certain Nicole had violated HR etiquette and possibly even some laws.

"Are there not *any* asset management administrators out there worth interviewing?" Nicole cried out.

"Hey, let me ask you something. Do we really need a permanent, on-site admin? I mean, is Robert really that busy?" Paul's wheels were turning, and Nicole could see something was happening; she knew to just follow his lead and see it through. "I'm just wondering. For what we've been paying Robert, who has caused us more problems and headaches than he's worth, we could probably get our consultant here one week a month."

Nicole's eyes lit up. "*Yes! That's it!*" she yelped. Nicole's sun was back out, and her rainbow was brightly colored.

A few weeks passed. Both Paul and Nicole had made inquiries, but no decision had been given. It was starting to look like it wasn't going to happen. To top it off, Robert's exit was just days away.

Now, during all of this, Nicole's favorite movie came out on DVD. Yes, *Talladega Nights*. She had seen it on opening night in the theater and twice thereafter. Ricky Bobby was her new best friend, and she couldn't wait to see him again at home on her own terms, where she could laugh as loud as she wanted without having to tone it down for the other moviegoers. Nicole loved everything about the movie, especially the quotes. You'd hear her spouting off in random conversations like she had *Talladega Nights* Tourette syndrome, "If you're not first, you're last", "I'll hold your hair", and even "Don't make me go spider monkey on your ass". Her all-time favorite quote from the movie, though, was "shake and bake". She'd say it every chance she got. "Shake and bake" this and "shake and bake" that. She'd say it to her team members during meetings as a way to agree with something and even to the CIO himself. Yes, Nicole was a *Talladega Nights* whore, and she was force-feeding it to all, forcing them to embrace it, too.

[NICOLE'S NOTE: *Will Ferrell and Adam McKay are brilliant writers. I loved this movie. I have two copies in case I break one from watching it so much.*]

Robert's last day was in three days. Nicole was starting to get antsy. Paul hadn't had any news yet on the executive board's decision about the consultant. She was sitting at her desk in her office, contemplating whether Jonathan and Pam were really as bad as they seemed, when Paul bum-rushed her office.

"What's going on? What's wrong?" Nicole said, surprised by Paul bursting in. She wondered if someone was in need of medical attention or at least a 911 call.

With just a cat grin on his face, Paul simply said, "We got him!"

In the loudest praise-voice Nicole could wail out, she sang, "*Eight pounds, six ounces!*"

Confused by this lesson on the measuring system, Paul cocked his head to the side and said, "What? What are you saying?"

"Eight pounds, six ounces!"

"What does that mean? I don't understand. Are you thirsty?" Paul responded, still confused.

Clarifying, Nicole finished the quote. "You know, eight-pound, six-ounce Baby Jesus! From *Talladega Nights*! It's my *favorite* part of the movie!"

"I thought 'shake and bake' was your favorite part!"

"It is, but there is this brilliant bit in the movie about Baby Jesus. Let me show you!" Nicole quickly YouTubed "Baby Jesus".

Together, Paul and Nicole laughed until their sides hurt. Nicole showed Paul all her favorite scenes and, before they knew it, they'd damn near watched the entire movie. Eight-pound, six-ounce Baby Jesus had been replayed over and over again.

"Oh my God, that's hilarious!! We've got to start using it!" Paul proposed.

"I've simply been waiting for the right time and right situation. You can only praise Baby Jesus when it's something really wonderful, and this was the perfect time!" Nicole confirmed.

From that point on, "eight pounds, six ounces" could be heard being shouted by either Paul or Nicole, and sometimes together, anytime something wonderful happened they knew involved divine intervention!

Appropriate Moments to Praise Baby Jesus

Everyone can fully understand and appreciate the need for a term that expresses your elation for those hallelujah moments when things work out your way. Those moments where you can relax, relate and release all of the built-up tension from waiting and worrying and finally being able to celebrate the accomplishment. When those moments occur, it's time to "eight pounds, six ounces" (Baby Jesus)!

Your hallelujah moment is more than just the words "eight pounds, six ounces". Praise must be given properly! Hands must go up, and the sentiment must be shared with a fellow Hoofer, or at least someone else who has seen *Talladega Nights*. Shake and bake!

[NICOLE'S NOTE: *Let me just go on record here on two topics. First, we are not, I repeat* not, *trying to convert anyone. Your religious preference is yours, so if you want to eight-pound, six-ounce Baby Allah, Baby Buddha, Baby "the messiah that is still to come" or any other eight-pound, six-ounce deity, you go right ahead! The point is to praise and be joyful that your whatever happened! Second, and this is especially important, I love* Talladega Nights*! Will Ferrell, if you are reading, I love you!*]
[PAUL'S NOTE: *Nicole, squirrel!*]
[NICOLE'S NOTE: *Oh yeah, well, I'm just sayin'. People, if you haven't seen it yet, buy it! Don't rent.* Buy! *You'll love it, too! I'm done.*]

Two more of our very favorite "eight pounds, six ounces" moments are because of food (we're sure you're not surprised). The first one Nicole discovered on her way to work one morning, and the other Paul and Nicole discovered together one day while they were having a "'shroom attack".

The Goodness

Pregnancy is an amazing rite of passage for a woman, or so Nicole thought. While many women had horrible pregnancies, Nicole rather enjoyed hers, so when she found out she was pregnant with her third child; she was overjoyed and looking forward to using the excuse of "eating for two" again. However, Nicole hadn't figured her age into the equation.

The first blow came with morning sickness. First, it was the fact that she had it at all. Second, it was more like all-day-long sickness. Once she realized the queasiness subsided when she snacked constantly, though, things turned around, and she turned to any chicken biscuit spot. She had every one mapped from her front door to the office and stopped there often.

The second blow was her sciatic nerve. The last two times she was pregnant, it acted up in her third trimester, when she was at her heaviest. This time, however, it started up when she was only four months pregnant and still quite thin.

[PAUL'S NOTE: *Wait, wait, wait. I know this is your story and your journey, but I see I'm going to have to slow your roll to keep you straight. While I fully support slight exaggerations when describing oneself, I can't let you get away with "quite thin". You were certainly not fat, but "quite thin"? Really?*]
[NICOLE'S NOTE: *All right, fine. Ladies, let me back this train up to give you the full picture.*]
[PAUL'S NOTE: *Beep. Beep.*]
[NICOLE'S NOTE: *Really, dumbass? Really? Anyway, when I had my first child, I was at my ideal weight and a ripe young age. When I had my second child, many years later, my doctor at the time had the audacity to say to me, "How much did you gain with your first child? Oh, fifty-three pounds? Well, you could stand to* lose *weight with this baby." WHAT THE HELL?! All I could think was that this biznatch just called me fat! And now here I was with my new doctor on baby number three when she goes, "Oh, you're just shy of your thirty-fifth birthday? Well, that's fine; plenty of my older mothers have children later in life, and they're just fine." Wait. The first beeeeotch called me fat, now this heffa's calling me old! WTH?! W-T-H?!*]

The third and final blow for Nicole was when she found out she had gestational diabetes. For a Hoofer, that's the kiss of death. Pre-baby, Nicole always enjoyed the corner piece of the monthly birthday cake. However, now it was only two-by-two squares with a little icing. The "no more sweet tea; try unsweet with artificial sweetener" comments made by the nutritionist were not only insulting, but cut like a knife being pushed through her heart. Nicole was a southern girl through and through, and no respectful southerner would put artificial sweetener in her tea!

Of course, Nicole is responsible, and she did what she had to do to ensure a happy, healthy baby girl, and that's just what she got. What she didn't get was the surge of energy she had after the first two were born. Just a few short weeks after Gabi was born, Nicole had to return to work, and every morning was a struggle just to get her hooves out of bed. Helping with homework, painting fingers and toes, and being a walking vending machine was a 24/7 job, and Nicole was done. D-O-N-E! Done!

On top of all that, Nicole had a husband who had needs as well, which often came in the middle of the night when no one was up.

[NICOLE'S NOTE: *Guys, while I'm sure the mere thought of your wife is enough to get your motor running, for a mother of a newborn, it takes a wee bit more foreplay to get us in the mood. Here's a technique that may help. Ready? It's called SLEEP! Yes, sleep is the best type of foreplay you can give your wife, girlfriend, or baby's mama. So during the week, foreplay it up! Then, on the weekend, call one of those "eager to babysit" friends of yours who swore if you ever needed someone she'd be there. Ship the baby (and any other kids) off to her house, and then you and your woman sleep some more, together. Trust me, by the time she wakes up, she'll be ready for the kind of lovin' you were getting pre-kids. Just remember: sleep equals sex. Waking us up in the middle of the night when the baby finally went to sleep after being up for hours equals no sex…for days!*]

[PAUL'S NOTE: *Pearls of wisdom, I see.*]

[NICOLE'S NOTE: *I'm just saying what millions of women are thinking. Oh yeah, one final note, women. If your man gets the hint and lets you sleep and then ships the kids off, take the hint and sex him up right! He engaged in the foreplay; now you need to be engaged in the sex!*]

At work, Nicole was dragging like a sixty-five-year-old's ass in a pair of hot pants, and she needed a pick-me-up. Unfortunately, the sweet tea in the cafeteria wasn't sweet enough (and you can't make cold sweet tea sweeter just by adding sugar), and she didn't like coffee. What was a thirty-something vixen to do?

[PAUL'S NOTE: *"Vixen" now?*]
[NICOLE'S NOTE: *If you don't stop, I'm going to knock you in the head and tell God you died! I already slowed my roll. You are getting on my last nerve with that, and I only have one left! I am a vixen. Married or not, mother or not, every woman should have a little vixen in her, and I definitely embrace mine!*]
[PAUL'S NOTE: *Very nice!*]
[NICOLE'S NOTE: *<sucks teeth and gives the "I know what that means" look>*]

She knew the answer: vanilla cappuccinos. Oh, they were delicious and sweet, and they had just the right amount of caffeine. The problem was the only place she'd ever had a good one was nowhere near her house or office. Finally, one day, unable to maintain her usual seventy-five miles per hour speed in a forty-five zone, Nicole pulled into the Loca Mocha gas station near her office and prayed for cappuccino.

As she walked in, she admired how the store was designed to have the look and feel of a NASCAR pit. Then, near the corrugated steel backsplash, Baby Jesus shined a light on a heavenly coffee dispenser with names like English Toffee, Caramel Macchiato and Cinnamon Roll. However, in the first position, under the brightest light (or so it seemed) was Vanilla Cappuccino. "Oh please, please, be as good as I remember it," Nicole thought. She grabbed a sixteen-ounce cup and hit the dispense button.

Goosebumps surfaced on her skin as she heard the motor running from the dispenser. It was hot and frothy. *Please, baby, baby, please*, was all she kept thinking. When it finished, she went to the counter, paid for the cappuccino, and drove to work.

[NICOLE'S NOTE: *A word to the wise. Never, ever drink the cappuccino as soon as it's poured unless you want to talk with a lisp the rest of the day because it will annihilate your tongue. I know; I speak from experience. Mmnt!*]

About twenty minutes after Nicole arrived, Paul heard it.

"*Eight pounds, six ounces!*"

Paul instant messaged Nicole. "OMG! What?"

"I have found it!" she replied. "I have found the Holy Grail of cappuccinos."

"What are you talking about?" Paul typed back.

"The Loca Mocha gas station around the corner makes the *best* vanilla cappuccinos I have *ever* had. Mmm, mmm, good!" Nicole responded, putting her spirit fingers in the air.

"OHHHH! I thought you were having a religious moment for a minute there, and I didn't want to intrude. Cool. I've never had one, but it sounds like you're happy as hell over there!" Paul cheered.

"Lord, yes! Baby Jesus just knew I wasn't going to make it today," Nicole enthusiastically responded with smiley faces and all, "and he shined his little heavenly light down and pulled me in. Hallelujah!"

Unfortunately, by midmorning, the cappuccino had worn off, and Nicole had an internal conversation about how the caffeine in the cappuccino was a lot like Chinese food: it's great when it first goes down but then wears off rather quickly. She needed another cup of coffee, and now all she had was the nasty generic brand in the break room. This was not going to do.

The next morning, Nicole stopped at the Loca Mocha again. She had found the Holy Grail, but it was somehow incomplete, and she had an idea on how to make it more holy. She added some premium coffee and some additional squirts of French vanilla concentrate! And with that, perfection was born. She had found the "goodness".

The morning passed quickly, and before Nicole knew it, it was lunchtime. The next day, she made the same concoction again, and it was lunchtime before her first yawn. *Yes!* She had found it! The baby could wake up a hundred times in a night, and she would be fine because she had been blessed with the recipe.

Eventually, Paul started noticing that Nicole always came in with a Loca Mocha cup. "Is it really that good?" he asked skeptically.

"Of course! I wouldn't be stopping every day if it weren't. Hello!" Realizing she needed to enlighten Paul, Nicole decided to bring him in a cup of goodness.

"What's this?" Paul questioned as Nicole glided by his desk and dropped off the blue-and-red cup one morning.

"Just drink," Nicole responded.

At first, all she heard was "Mmnt!" as she continued down the hall. And then, *"Eight pounds, six ounces!"*

She simply smiled. Yes, Baby Jesus had heard her prayers and sent the good stuff to the Loca Mocha. No more sleepy mornings and no more cranky moods. Nope, she, and now Paul, would be bright-eyed and bushy-tailed from here on out!

A few days after incorporating the goodness into his morning routine, Paul approached Nicole hesitantly.

"Hey, do you have a sec?" Paul asked quietly.

"Sure, what's up, sweetie?" Nicole responded, turning around in her chair and seeing Paul sitting on her desk.

"You know I love the goodness, but man, I gotta tell you, the goodness does not love me," Paul whispered.

"What do you mean?" Nicole replied, lowering her voice as well.

"Well, let's just say the goodness leaves about as quickly as it goes in every morning. You know how you were talking about wanting me to do a cleanse with you? Let's just say there's no need now."

Laughing, Nicole said, "Honey, I used to be that way with coffee, but it won't last long. Give it another couple of weeks, and you'll be back to normal."

"No, that's not what I want either!" Paul said, shocked.

"I'm confused then," Nicole questioned.

"As long as it's normal, I don't want the morning cleanse to stop! I like feeling thin." With that, Paul stood up, turned sideways, and showed Nicole the concavity of his stomach. "See, it's great! The goodness is not only heavenly, but it even makes you skinny. I love it!"

"You are stupid. You'll pudge right back up in a couple of weeks. Mark my words. The jiggly will be back."

"Really?"

"Really," Nicole said, frowning. "Look at me. If it were true, I'd be wasted away to nothing by now."

"Yes, good point. You don't look any thinner," Paul teased.

"Bitch 'bout to get cut," Nicole deadpanned, arching an eyebrow.

"Okay, okay. I'm just kidding. Me and my thinness are going back to my desk," Paul mocked, purposely sucking in his stomach and pretending to have to hold his pants up with his hands.

Unamused, Nicole bid Paul farewell with a frosty, "Good decision."

We're not sure exactly why we're choosing to share this secret formula with you because we know as soon as you read it, you're going to run right out and get some, leaving none for us. However, having this coffee in the morning does indeed always make us raise our little hooves and praise Baby Jesus, so we're hoping you thieving whores will be kind enough to leave some for us.

Without further ado, here is the secret Loca Mocha "Goodness" formula! Fill a sixteen-ounce cup in this order:

1. Three complete squirts of French vanilla concentrate.
2. Three ounces of premium coffee (in other words, fill it to the first ridge in the cup); swirl it and the French vanilla concentrate together until well mixed.
3. Fill the rest of the cup with French vanilla cappuccino. Stir gently, add the top, and your pit stop is complete. You're off to the races and a great start to your day. Sip carefully, though, because Loca Mocha's coffee is hot! *Eight pounds, six ounces!*

Key Lime Cheesecake

Paul and Nicole couldn't have discovered Key lime cheesecake at a better time. When they left their last job, they also left behind their weekly pilgrimages to their favorite cheesecake establishment because there wasn't one close by anymore. Oh, how they missed their white chocolate caramel macadamia nut cheesecake and their pumpkin pecan cheesecake (offered only during the holidays).

[PAUL'S NOTE: *And our hooves were at half-mast for weeks as we mourned the loss of our weekly cheesecake.*]
[NICOLE'S NOTE: *Do you think they would ship me a pumpkin pecan cheesecake every month instead of just during the holidays if I placed an order now and begged?*]
[PAUL'S NOTE: *Nicole, squirrel.*]
[NICOLE'S NOTE: *I'm writing myself a reminder now. Carry on.*]

The day of discovery had been especially trying for Nicole. That morning, her youngest daughter, Gabi, had spit up all over her, and it wasn't the kind you could just grab a baby wipe and clean up on the go. No, it was the down-the-front, onto-the-pants, and into-the-shoes kind of spit-up.

[NICOLE'S NOTE: *Ladies, I know you feel me here. Can I get an "Amen!"?*]

Annoyed, Nicole went back upstairs to find something to change into. Now normally, pre-baby, this wouldn't have been an arduous task, but Nicole hadn't quite lost those twenty pounds of baby weight she'd gained. Finding another outfit was going to be tricky. She only had a handful of outfits she could still wear that didn't show off her unwanted assets (you know, those extra rolls and back fat she had acquired).

After twenty minutes, she finally found an outfit that made her look less like a stuffed sausage and more like lean turkey (voluptuous in all the right places). She ironed it, threw it on, picked up the baby (spit cloth intact), grabbed her other daughter, Autumn, and headed out.

When she made it into work, she caught a disapproving glare from her manager. Then, the project manager she'd been working with for the last couple of months tried to throw her under the bus and claim the slowdown on the project was her fault because he'd provided all the information and she was just sitting on it.

[NICOLE'S NOTE: *And let me tell you (wait—let me start my neck roll now), that bus was coming at ninety miles an hour and didn't care who it clipped. Those four tires mowed me down and squashed me before I even saw that big yellow sonofabitch coming!*]

Nicole was stuck trying to be professional and still save her team's reputation. Since it was the CIO who asked about the slowdown, her manager was on edge. And when he's on edge, he's on Nicole's ass like white on rice.

Nicole labored all morning on a painstakingly anal retentive e-mail that carefully detailed the dates and times she'd delivered *every task* to the out-of-control, bus-driving project manager. When she was done, she not only cleared her team's besmirched name, but she also showed the project manager for what he was: the driver of a carnival VW Bug (aka a clown)!

Nicole was done! D-O-N-E! Done! She'd had the morning from hell and needed to feel comforted. She got up from her desk and headed over to Paul, leaving her lunch box lonely and feeling inadequate. When she reached Paul's desk, she simply said, "You ready?"

"Yeah. I guess this means we're going out for lunch, huh?" Paul asked.

"Yes, yes it does. I've had a horrible day. I need some love; some big, fat, cheesy pizza love. So let's hit the place up the street so I can get my carb on!" Nicole ordered.

Never one to stifle a fellow Hoofer in need, Paul simply nodded and got up from his seat, wallet in hand.

As Nicole pulled into the parking lot, Baby Jesus smiled down upon her and shone a single beam of sunlight on a store sign she'd never seen before, hidden behind the pizza parlor. It simply said "Bakery". She looked over at Paul and whispered, "Eight pounds, six ounces. We'll be stopping there before we go back." Paul looked over and was awestruck. How had he never seen that before? How had he missed those six glorious letters?

"Am I losing my dessert-dar?" he pondered as they entered the restaurant.

Nicole distracted Paul with her stories over pizza and pretzel rolls.

[PAUL'S NOTE: *Uh, and your large sweet tea. I know you were in distress, and I'm not judging, but don't yada yada the tea. For the record, I had water.*]

[NICOLE'S NOTE: *Really?*]

Once Nicole had purged the bad juju of the morning out of her system, they headed to the store simply titled "Bakery" in hopes of salvation. Inside, they were not disappointed. They were treated to an assortment of cupcakes, cookies, and cheesecakes. Everywhere they turned was a confection worthy of an "eight pounds, six ounces" moment. They settled on a slice of something called Key lime cheesecake, intrigued at the thought of the combined flavors, and ordered it to go.

Around three o'clock that afternoon, it was time for tea…and cheesecake. Tina had declined that day, so Paul and Nicole were secretly thrilled they only had to split their new dessert two ways.

They unwrapped the cheesecake, careful to not let *any* stick to the wax paper, and they prepared their forks for attack.

[PAUL'S NOTE: *Don't laugh. You true dessert whores out there know what we're talking about. Wax paper, even though it's not supposed to, can rob you of precious toppings and crust if you let it. Peel carefully.*]

Simultaneously, Paul and Nicole lowered their forks, making sure their first bites included the whipped topping, the cheesecake, and the crust. They lifted and inserted. Without warning, they both jerked forward.

"Oh my God! My spit glands just went crazy! Did you feel it, too? Those spit glands near the base of my throat just spasmed like a snake with venom!" Nicole writhed, closing her eyes to fully enjoy the moment.

"Mine, too!" Paul exclaimed. "This is the best cheesecake I've ever had. Eight-pound, six-ounce Baby Jesus was looking after you today!"

"He was indeed, and he has washed away my cares with this cheesecake," Nicole said joyously. Narrowing her eyes, she continued, "Now, I'm going to need you to back away slowly and leave me and *my* cheesecake alone. My troubles are too heavy for half a slice to cure."

"Scuse me?" came Paul's reply as he changed the position of the fork in hand to look like a weapon. "You know better than to tease me about my dessert. Bitch 'bout to get stabbed."

Deadlocked for a moment, Nicole finally relented, knowing Paul was probably half serious. After all, hell hath no wrath like a dessert whore scorned, and Nicole had already scorned enough people that day.

Like all good things, though, teatime and cheesecake came to an end. Think back to the days when you were a little kid and your parents took you to the house of someone who had some cool toy you always wanted but never got; maybe that thing was a pony, an Atari, a big Barbie playhouse with all the furniture and the pool for the backyard, or the complete set of GI Joe or He-Man action figures. Whatever it was, do you remember the feeling you had when your parents told you it was time to leave Neverland? That feeling that you didn't want to leave and wished those parents could adopt you so you could live forever with "it"? That's the feeling Paul and Nicole shared as they left the cafeteria that day. They had just consumed the best piece of cheesecake in their short, young lives and were having to leave it all behind and return to the reality of it all, without any more Key lime cheesecake.

[NICOLE'S NOTE: *Like how I threw "young" in there for us?*]
[PAUL'S NOTE: *Well, for me, it's actually true.*]
[NICOLE'S NOTE: *Really? You are only a little younger than me!*]
[PAUL'S NOTE: *Younger. That's the key word. And thusly less wrinkled and more attractive.*]
[NICOLE'S NOTE: *Very nice!*]

Randomly over the next few weeks, Paul and Nicole popped into the bakery, hoping to catch their favorite new cheesecake sitting lonely behind the window, just waiting to be picked up and eaten.

[NICOLE'S NOTE: *Sounds like the plight of every woman.*]
[PAUL'S NOTE: *OMG, did you just go there?*]
[NICOLE'S NOTE: *Yes, yes I did. Ladies, can I get another "Amen!"?*]

For whatever reason, they were always unsuccessful. Paul began hounding the bakery day in and day out until finally, one shiny day, Nicole heard Paul cry out, "Eight pounds, six ounces!" Without another word, she knew what it meant, and she was at his cube, keys in her hand, ready to Ricky Bobby it on over to the bakery. Only this time, like in the old commercial selling the eighties R and B love songs, she quickly flickered the words out to Paul like the serpent flickers its tongue, "No, no, no, my brotha. You've gotta get your own! We won't be sharing any of this goodness."

Arriving at the bakery in record time, Paul and Nicole explained the situation and the dire need for them to have Key lime cheesecake every week. The bakery agreed to offer it on Fridays, and to this day, Paul and Nicole have never missed their weekly pilgrimage to Key lime cheesecake heaven.

[PAUL'S NOTE: *This is the only time we don't share a dessert. Every other time, we always pick something we both like and share it to save on the calories and guilt, but on Fridays, it's every man and woman for themselves with a large slice of the divine Key lime cheesecake. Thank you, Baby Jesus. Eight pounds, six ounces!*]

Trimming the Fat

In today's world, everyone is looking for the team player. Not only should you celebrate yourself, but celebrate the accomplishments of those around you. Give credit where credit is due, and you will always shine (just like the glaze on a Krispy Kreme doughnut when the "Hot" sign is on).

Very Nice

Meaning

The best thing you can say when someone makes an obviously untrue statement you can't prove.

Heart of the Story ♥

This one is Paul's, though Paul and Nicole's friend, Tina, cemented it into infamy.

As we've said, Tina is our very beautiful, blonde, mature friend. Don't you hate it when people say *mature*? We do, too, but Tina just simply can't be called old. It'd be like calling a '54 Corvette Roadster, painted in its original rare Sportsman Red paint, just a car. No, she's in a class all her own and continues to appreciate in value as she ages gracefully.

Did we also mention that she talks really, really fast? So fast that in many cases, when she joins us for lunch or for afternoon tea, we often just end up listening to her, nodding in agreement, and smiling politely at all her Tina-isms. Another reminder that if you ever see us, you have to remind us to tell you about "FF". It's too graphic for this book but, oh my God, she had us on the floor with that one.

Tail

One afternoon we were taking our usual fifteen-minute tea break in the cafeteria. It's nothing elaborate like you British people have. It's not served to us on a silver tray by a butler who stands around and asks, "One lump or two?" (Or at least that's how we imagine it's done over there. If it's not, don't burst our bubble.) No, we use little eight ounce Styrofoam cups, which were downgraded from ten ounces a few months back due to budget cuts. (Really?) We fill them with hot water from the coffee pot that only dispenses water in a slow drizzle. We are extremely happy it had a water filter added to it a while back, so now our tea tastes more like tea and less gritty.

Paul, Nicole, and Tina went to their usual corner of the cafeteria. Their table was far enough away from everything and everyone else that it made the very obvious "Private meeting; do not intrude!" statement. Tea time was later in the afternoon, usually around 3:00 p.m., when everyone else had finished lunch and should have been back at their desks, slaving away. Occasionally, though, others were in the large cafeteria, also in hushed conversation. Acknowledgements from both sides, consisting of simple smiles and head nods, would occur, acknowledging the "don't want to be bothered" sentiment.

Tea time was rarely about work. It was often about things going on in one another's personal lives. From time to time, though, the occasional work-related drama had to be vented about in order to salvage the rest of the day. But mostly, it was like story time at your favorite bookstore that left your cheeks sore from laughter.

[NICOLE'S NOTE: *Laughter is the key to a healthy life, so help your friends be healthier, and buy this book for them as a gift. Not only will it improve their life, but it will also support my lipo fund. Fabulous at forty, ya'll!*]
[PAUL'S NOTE: *A-N-Y-W-A-Y!*]

[NICOLE'S NOTE: *Whatever, Paul! Don't even act like you wouldn't get a little lipo if this book became a bestseller and we ended up on Ellen Degeneres's couch! You know you'd be the first in line!*]
[PAUL'S NOTE: *(teeth-sucking sound)*]
[NICOLE'S NOTE: *Game, set, match! (happy dance)*]

Just like every other day, Paul, Nicole, and Tina took their "assigned" seats and settled into their conversation. Somehow, they got on the subject of aging. Nicole, being of mixed race, has beautiful café-au-lait skin, as she calls it, and those crows haven't even started trying to find a place to land near her eyes yet. Paul and Tina are pasty and white, however, and the buzzards are now circling and the crows are starting to land, so aging is an important topic.

The conversation went down the road of actresses who have aged well. You know, Lynn Whitfield, Michelle Pfeifer, Angela Basset, Cheryl Ladd, Diane Keaton and Olivia Newton-John.

[NICOLE'S NOTE: *Who Paul has loved since she donned those skin-tight, black hot pants and strutted her stuff in* Grease.]
[PAUL'S NOTE: OMG! MILF! Hump Island!]
[PAUL'S NOTE: *For those of you who haven't heard of Hump Island, that's your list of five actors or actresses who you and your significant other have agreed you can have your way with should the opportunity ever arise.*]

"Yeah, like, did you know Lynn Whitfield is in her sixties?!" Nicole asked.

Paul and Tina simultaneously responded, "Who?"

"Typical white people!" Now, Nicole felt that because she was both African American and German that she could make whatever racial comment she wanted and get away with it. And quite frankly, she often did! "Did either of you see *The Josephine Baker Story*? It was an HBO movie."

Paul, unaffected by Nicole's slur, said, "Oh yeah! I remember that movie!"

"Well of course you would. Young, hot mocha latté dancing around topless with bananas around her waist. Mmnt! Anyway, the chick who played Josephine is Lynn Whitfield. She's absolutely beautiful and is aging so gracefully!"

"Well, have you seen Christie Brinkley?!" Paul countered. "I tell you what, she still rivals many of today's twenty-something models. I would have *never* guessed she is in her sixties! She could get it!"

"When I was in my forties, people would always say I looked like I was in my twenties," Tina declared suddenly.

"Very nice," Paul retorted, looking over at her briefly and then continuing on with his sentence. After he finished, they sat in stunned silence as Nicole and Tina just looked at him. Nicole was in awe that Paul just shut Tina down on her comment, and Tina was left confused as to whether or not she'd just gotten dissed.

"Did you just say 'very nice'?" Nicole asked.

"Yeah. We didn't know Tina when she was in her forties, so we can't prove she didn't look like she was in her twenties, so I just 'very niced' her and moved on."

"What do you mean, you 'very niced' me?" Tina replied, speaking even higher and faster than normal.

"'Very nice' is a phrase you can use any time you don't want to challenge someone on an obviously untrue statement that you really can't prove. I've used it dozens of times, and it always works."

"So, you don't believe that I looked like I was in my twenties when I was in my forties?" Tina challenged, cocking her left eyebrow.

"Well, I can't prove that you didn't, so I just think that's very nice for you," Paul retorted, cocking his own right eyebrow in defense.

By now, Nicole was in ROFLWMM mode and making a scene, and their quiet afternoon tea had turned into an Alabama backyard barbecue.

[PAUL'S NOTE: *I'm allowed to say that because I'm from Alabama. I've lived it.*]

"Oh my God, oh my God, OH MY GOD! That is the funniest thing I have ever seen!" Nicole screamed. "When Tina said she looked like she was twenty, you just looked over at her, slipped in your 'very nice,' and just kept rolling like there was nothing unusual. That was smooth. I can't wait to try it out myself!"

"Let's see how you both do then," Paul tested. "Five years ago, when I was twenty-four, I was thirty pounds thinner and, yes, quite esurient all the time. Women lined up for my attention, but I just showed them my wedding ring and gave them the look that meant, 'That's right, you could have had all this, but it's too late.'"

"Very nice," they both chimed in unison, clearly pleased they'd grasped the concept so quickly. Then, Nicole, always full of piss and vinegar, added, "And five years ago, you weren't twenty-four, because that would mean you're twenty-nine now, and we both know you're not, dumbass. So I'm only 'very nicing' the part about you being thinner."

"Mmnt! Maybe that was a little too much. However, you know I only celebrate the anniversary of my twenty-ninth birthday so, to me, I am still that age."

"Whatever."

Feeling rebuked, Paul ended the conversation. "Okay, ladies, it's been real and it's been fun, but it hasn't been real fun. I need to get back."

Tea was over, but "very nice" lived on.

Very Nice Yourself Out of Any Situation

This cute little phrase will come in handy on many occasions. Below are some examples to help you understand when "very nice" is appropriate. Use it wisely.

1. Your boss suggests a solution that, if he'd just thought through a little longer, he would see is utterly useless. However, you know you're going to get stuck trying it anyway, no matter what you say. Very nice.
2. Your coworker declares her clothes are getting too loose because of the new diet she's on, but that camel toe she's been sporting is just as big and ugly as it was two weeks ago. Very nice.
3. The office resource hog brags about an "in" she has with a certain VP, and you know it's only because she's making him a box lunch at the Y every Thursday. Very nice.

[PAUL'S NOTE: *For those of you unfamiliar with the term, use our handy-dandy Glossary at the end of the book. I hate to say it twice.*]

4. Your coworker who is constantly out of the office on sick leave casually mentions he's already gotten his vacation approved for the last two weeks of the year, meaning your ass will have to be on call or in the office. Very nice.

Trimming the Fat

You've heard the old adages "You get more flies with honey" and "If you can't say something nice, don't say anything at all" and they're both true (unless you're with a fellow hoofer; then you can let it all hang out…except your chub…always keep that in check). Have a handy saying like "very nice" in your back pocket at all times to help curb your attitude and keep you from getting kicked to the curb.

Whore
(The very best word in the English language)

Meaning

Sure, we all know what a whore is, but that's not what we're talking about here. If we want to talk about those who are free with their bodies, then we call them a "ho" or a "skank-ass ho." For guys, we call them "lucky". No, to us, whores are those who love something greatly or who give themselves over to something freely.

Heart of the Story

Paul has used this word for years. Forgetting it's not a word in everyone's everyday vernacular, though, he sometimes uses it a little too often or in the presence of people who don't have the same relationship with the word he does. It is, without a doubt, the very best and most useful word in the English language.

Tail

As we've mentioned, Paul has three children. The middle one is Ryan, and he's the cutest little blonde-haired, blue-eyed thing you've ever seen. Oh, and he's thin as a rail. Paul and his wife, Marilyn, aren't sure where that comes from, although they each try to claim it's from their own side of the family. Ryan can have his little hooves as high in the air as he wants with whatever food he wants, and he doesn't gain a pound. He has to wear "slim" pants, and he frequently and proudly flaunts his little six-pack. Mmnt!

Not that we're not proud of him, you understand. In fact, it's great…for him.

However, Paul is still bitter from his younger days when the word "husky" was thrown around frequently in his presence. He and his mom flew to Texas every summer to visit his grandmother, and she would always take him to this mall that sold husky jeans. It's unclear why husky jeans couldn't be found closer to home, but no, they had to go all the way to Texas to find the huskies. It wasn't so bad that they were huskies because, when you're younger and you're a guy, weight isn't something you really obsess about all that much. What Paul did obsess about, though, was the fact that those jeans had an unusual color. They weren't the classic blue or the more trendy faded blue jeans of the time. No, that would have been too easy. The rinse on these jeans was so dark that they were purple. P-U-R-P-L-E! The first couple of times they were washed, Paul's mom had to wash them separately so they didn't stain anything else. To make matters worse, when Paul wore the knees out, his mom patched them with the denim knee patches you bought from the store. What was wrong with that, you ask? Nothing, except they don't make patches in purple! So his purple jeans lasted up until about Christmas each year. Then, inevitably, one by one, he would tear a hole in one of the knees during PE. After that, he came to school in purple jeans with blue patches on the knees. So having a son who is the extreme polar opposite and wears slim jeans is a bit of a bitter pill for Paul to swallow.

Anyway, Paul and his family were at a local Mexican restaurant having dinner one night. You know, the kind where you tell them what kind of burrito to make you, and it's so big you have to eat it with both hands. Hooves High! By default, these burritos came with tortilla chips, so to save space on their plates, the restaurant just combined all of their chips onto a separate plate. During the meal, Paul and Marilyn were talking about their days and having the usual conversations: homework, plans for the weekend, skank-hos, etc. Marilyn reached over to grab a chip, and the plate was empty.

"What happened to all the chips? Did they fall?" Marilyn asked. She began looking under and beside the table for the mess she was sure she would have to clean up.

"No," came a small, timid voice from next to Paul.

"Well, what happened then?" Marilyn asked.

"I ate them. I guess I'm a chip whore," Ryan responded, slowly yet matter-of-factly.

"You're a *what?*" Paul said, looking down at his son.

"A chip whore. I love these chips. I couldn't help myself!" Ryan beamed, a smile tugging at the corners of his lips.

"Oh my God, that is hilarious!" Paul burst out laughing. Everyone in the restaurant turned and stared.

In between laughing, Paul yelled to the other patrons, "It's okay. My son's a chip whore. I'm so proud!"

Mortified, Marilyn just stared at Paul, eyes wide with embarrassment. Brennan, their oldest daughter, started giggling.

"I want to be a chip whore, too!" she screamed.

"Shhh! Not you, too!" Marilyn sternly whispered. "You see what all these years of whore talk have done? Now your children have picked it up!"

[PAUL'S NOTE: *Don't you love how your significant other always refers to them as* your *children when they do something bad? Mmnt!*]

"Oh, come on, it's hilarious! He's only six; he doesn't even know what he's saying! Ryan, it's okay. You can be a chip whore. Brennan and I are dessert whores, and your mom is a meat and potatoes whore. We're all whores!"

"What are you saying? Stop it! What if they say that in school?" Marilyn's eyes reached cosmic proportions.

"Okay, okay," Paul said, calming down. "Kids, technically 'whore' is not a nice word, so you can't say it outside our family. Got it?"

"Yes, sir," they both replied quickly.

"See, they get it," Paul said with a smile to his wife.

"Mmnt!" was her only response.

Secretly, Paul high-fived Ryan and Brennan under the table and beamed proudly at his young son, who had mastered the art of whore talk at such a young age.

There's A Little Bit of Whore in you, Too

Everybody is a whore for something. Whether it's a dessert whore, like Paul, or a shoe whore, like Nicole, we know you give it up and give it freely to something more than you should. And why shouldn't you? If you believe that every detail of a project requires a face-to-face encounter, then you're a meeting whore. You like oral stimulation, and that's okay. Just be sure that when you open your mouth, you get to the point. A meeting without a climax or final decision at the end is a poor meeting indeed and leaves everyone unsatisfied.

If you're an online gamer who buys the latest quad-core processor or the newest graphics card to improve your *World of Warcraft* experience, be a proud computer whore. Repeat after us: "I give it freely and hard to the latest piece of technology. I wear that bitch out and go down and check her processing power all the time!"

If you want to be a vacation whore who gives yourself over to the pleasures of vacationing in tropical lands, go for it! Let the sand and sun have their way with you. Let the waves whip your body and the salty breezes caress your neck and arms. Just remember to cover it up while you're playing so no one gets burned.

If you like to get your manis and your pedis cured, and the thought of a stranger sloughing the dead skin off your feet sends chills of anticipation down your spine, you are a nail whore. Let their toys of torture deliver pleasure to your extremities and leave a lasting imprint you gladly show off to all your family and friends.

If you are a young woman who prefers to dress in seductive or suggestive fashion, especially in a style based on a schoolgirl image, then you are a kinderwhore. Let it go.

Finally, if you're the kind who sleeps around or unabashedly flirts with someone else's man or woman, you're a shameless whore. If you do all that, and you're *also* married, then you're a stupid whore, and you deserve everything you have coming to you. We're just sayin'… karma's a bitch, and she's taking names and keeping score.

[NICOLE'S NOTE: *I have a great story about that, but it's a whole other book. Mmnt!*]

Trimming the Fat

Don't be afraid to live outside the box. If you're stuck doing something you don't like, talk to people who are living their dream, and find out how you can, too. Do you, and do it to the best of your ability. As long as it's legal, own it, flaunt it, and work it. When you find a way to do what you love, your spirit will be full (just like a twenty-four-layer piece of chocolate cake).

Really?

Meaning

Any time you know the line or story someone is giving you is a hot mess, or any time you find yourself in a situation you can't believe is really happening.

Heart of the Story

We recognize that "really" isn't a new word. It's been around for ages, so we're not trying to take credit for it. However, we will take credit for the tone in which this version of "really" is used.

You see, there are various interpretations of "Really?" Their intent is based on the inflection of your voice. For instance, when you say, "Really?" in a high-pitched tone, it suggests excitement and/or surprise. Your friend just tells you that she's got two buddy passes to LA for the weekend and that one's for you. Your "REALLY?" answer is quite appropriate and lets her know you're happy. However, by simply changing the tone of your voice and adding a bit of emphasis, "Really?" takes on a whole new meaning.

By holding the *r* for just a second longer than normal and accompanying it with a little sideways glance and head tilt, "Really?" easily turns into a sarcastic and rhetorical comment that tells listeners that they or the situation they're in are stupid. For instance, let's say you're a little sluggish today, and when you stop by the break room for your second cup of coffee, there is an empty coffeepot sitting on the warmer. Really?

[PAUL'S NOTE: *To be honest, your dumb ass should have just gone to the Loca Mocha before coming to work and made yourself a coffee using the secret formula, but maybe now you've learned your lesson. Mmnt.*]

"Really?" can also be substituted for other commonly used phrases like "Seriously?" or "Are you kidding me?" or "WTH?" or "WTF?"

Tail

Okay, we promised you this tail earlier, and here it is. We affectionately call it "What Happens in Vegas, Breaks in Vegas". Yes, Paul and Nicole went to Vegas on a natural high, sure that Lady Luck was on their side and ready to reward them handsomely. What they didn't know was that Lady Luck was a vindictive bitch who intended to slap them down and then kick them to the curb. By the end of their trip, they were forced to reinvent their use of the common, everyday word "really".

[NICOLE'S NOTE: *Now this was before I was christened the Oracle by Jeffrey, because if I had known I had those powers, I would have predicted it was going to be one of the craziest weeks of our lives (and to bring more comfortable shoes).*]

Every year, there is a huge conference, primarily for IT people, who develop and implement processes (which is exactly what Paul and Nicole do).

[PAUL & NICOLE'S NOTE: *And quite well, we'd like to add.*]

This particular year, the conference was in Las Vegas, and Paul and Nicole got approved to go, much to their delight. People in the office, aware of the trouble they tend to get into together, rolled their eyes, and Paul and Nicole flaunted their upcoming trip as much as possible.

"Did you hear that Paul and I are going to Vegas for the IT conference?" Nicole would casually throw into her conversations. "Yeah, we're excited to spend a whole week learning about the latest trends in process management." And then, turning sideways and looking back at her audience, she'd whisper, "But, giiirrrrl, you know I'm gonna tear up that town at night! We're going during the week of the NBA All Stars, and you know this hot café-au-lait mama is gonna be looking at all that dark chocolate!"

Paul, equally affected, would interject small quips here and there to his team, such as, "I hate it that that project is going live while I'll be gone," or, "I know you've got this and won't need me the week I'm in Vegas. I'll be so busy, you understand."

[PAUL'S NOTE: *Looking back at all that preening we did, I wonder if it was indeed karma that kicked our asses and not Vegas herself, but I guess it doesn't really matter now. We made it back in one piece. Mostly.*]

Their first clue things might not have been as grand as Paul and Nicole wanted came when they booked their hotel. The conference hotel on the Strip was sold out of discounted rooms but, not being ones to complain or beg, Paul and Nicole offered to stay at a less expensive hotel on the Strip that offered rooms at the same rate. It was just a couple of hotels down from where the conference was, so they figured they'd just walk back and forth each day, convincing themselves it would allow them to eat at all the buffets they wanted without gaining a pound.

[PAUL'S NOTE: *Remember the rules of caloric accumulation, people!*]

The plane ride to Vegas was great. Because the trip took longer than three hours, their company booked them in business class and they so appreciated the smug swiping of the curtain from the flight attendant that separated them from the common herd. Yes, Paul and Nicole were the bulls, and the heffas were in the back. They leaned back, fluffed their pillows, watched a movie, and enjoyed the constant supply of little cookies the flight attendants were more than happy to bring. Hooves High!

Because their conference began so early on Monday, Paul and Nicole arrived on Sunday to get settled in. As they stepped off the plane, they looked back apologetically at the heffas in coach and gave them a little wave indicating their time would come soon.

Day One: Sunday

When they entered the terminal, they were dazzled by the slot machines, huge TV screens, and mirrored glass everywhere.

After baggage claim, Paul and Nicole headed outside, where they drew in deep breaths of the warm, dry, desert air. It felt electric, and as they slipped on their sunglasses and motioned for a taxi, they knew this was going to be their lucky week. They were either going to come back rich or ten pounds lighter (because, after all, it was NBA playoff weekend, and they intended to catch as many of those parties as they could and dance the night away).

Traffic seemed to magically part for them as they zipped along to their hotel, and within fifteen minutes they were being escorted into its huge lobby and beckoned by one of its pleasant minions. Everything was in order and ready for them and, as they headed to their rooms to change, their moods couldn't have been better. Paul unlocked his hotel room door, went inside, and suddenly everything changed.

He was immediately assaulted by the abundance of frayed carpet that greeted him at his entryway. Stepping over the carpet afro, he ventured on, thinking, *Really, no one has reported that?* When he flipped on the lights, another surprise was waiting. Peeled wallpaper. *Okay*, he thought, *this must be a joke. For $275 a night, I can't believe they have peeling wallpaper. Really?*

Determined not to let his poor accommodations ruin his trip, he began unpacking. As he took his toiletries into the bathroom, the faint smell of mold tickled his nose. Looking around, he noticed more wrinkled wallpaper, this time darker than the rest. "What's this? Mold? Greeaaatt. I can't wait to hear how Nicole's room looks." With that, he freshened up and went back to the bedroom to watch TV until it was time to meet Nicole.

The hotel guide flicked on and tempted Paul with lots of great choices, but each time he made a selection or changed the channel, nothing happened. He checked the remote for batteries. They were there, but he took a couple of spare AAs he had in his laptop bag and replaced them just to be sure. (IT guys always travel with spare AAs.) Still nothing. He tried the old school method of changing the channels on the TV. Nothing. *Mmnt. This is not happening*, he thought, and he turned off the TV and headed down to the lobby to wait for Nicole.

"So, tell me about your room!" Paul barked as soon as Nicole was in sight.

"Oh, it's very nice. I've got everything all set up. My hooves are high! Let's eat!" And Nicole headed off down the path the buffet sign pointed them in.

"Wait, wait, wait," Paul said, stopping her. "Your room doesn't have any issues?"

"Issues? No. It's just a hotel room. Why?"

"Mmnt!"

Laughing, she asked, "Why did you say that? Is something wrong with yours?"

"*Yes!* I have frayed carpet, peeling wallpaper, mold in my bathroom, and my TV won't get off the guide channel!" Paul exclaimed quickly.

"What? Are you kidding? Really?"

"Yes, really!"

"Are you sure you know how to operate the remote?"

"Don't insult my intelligence. I am in IT!"

[PAUL'S NOTE: *Never, I repeat never, try to tell someone in IT they can't work an electronic device. Even if we've never seen it before, we all know we were just born with the innate knowledge needed to work it.*]

"Okay, well, you'll have to show me later. Mama is hungry and needs some food!"

Laughing, Paul agreed, "All right. Let's go strap on our feed bags."

When they arrived at the buffet entrance, the heavens opened and the angels sang. Acres of glorious food and a huge pasture of desserts were waiting for them.

[NICOLE'S NOTE: *And let me tell you, Paul would have slapped his mama naked to get inside and get his hands on those desserts!*]

As usual, Paul returned from his first trip with a small plate of entrées and vegetables—and two precariously balanced plates of dessert.

"Oh my God, they have everything!" he oinked in delight. "My hooves are high!"

"Yes, and there is no judging tonight, agreed?" Nicole added, glancing down at her own mammoth plates of shrimp, crab claws, and steak.

"Agreed!" And with that, nary a word was spoken as they began to build the Great Wall of China out of their empty plates.

After their feast, Nicole wanted to walk the Strip and see the sights. Paul concurred that they both needed the exercise, so they set off, Nicole in her cutest of shoes, ready to be discovered.

There were a total of twelve hotels they wanted to see on the main 2.5-mile Strip, but after they passed the first few, Nicole needed a break.

"Damn, are we done yet? I am tired!" she declared.

Laughing, Paul said, "No, this is only our fourth hotel. We've got eight more."

"Eight! Are you kidding me?" Nicole bellyached. "I can't be cute for eight more hotels! Do you see these heels?"

"What if your Minnesota Timberwolf, Kevin Garnett, is at the last hotel? You know he's on the all-star roster, right?"

"Good point. Press on," Nicole said, straightening up and sucking it in. "Hang on, let me reapply. My lipstick could be fading."

As they continued, Paul noticed that Nicole was getting slower and slower. "Would you come on? It's going to be midnight before we finish."

"I am trying to hold it together and be cute, but my feet are *killing* me! I haven't been able to feel my toes since the last hotel, and now I have a searing pain going up my legs and thighs. I don't think I can go on!" She sat down. "I'm sorry, Kevin," she said to no one while looking up at the sky. "If you're out there, you'll never know what you're missing."

"Really? It's that bad?"

"Look at me. When have I ever given up on anything? I am telling you I am done. D-O-N-E. Done."

"Okay, let's go to the lobby of this hotel and talk to their minions about transportation back to our hotel."

To their surprise, there was a monorail close by that could take them back. Once onboard, Nicole did the unthinkable and removed her shoes.

"Are you crazy?" Paul scream-whispered. "Do you know the amount of filthiness and germs on this floor? Not to mention the vomit particles from all those drunk people who tossed their cookies once this tram started moving. Gross!"

"You know what?"

"What?"

"Bite me," Nicole said, obviously in pain. "I can't go another step in these torturous heels. Look at my feet. You can physically see my toes throbbing."

Nicole had begun limping as soon as they crossed the threshold of their hotel, so Paul helped her to her room.

[PAUL'S NOTE: *You are so transparent. You just wanted some rich, hot chocolate gentleman to see you limping and come swooping over and offer to pay some minions to pamper you.*]

[NICOLE'S NOTE: *Yes, yes I did.*]

After Paul escorted Nicole back to her room, he mentally prepared himself to reenter his project penthouse. "Good luck," Nicole threw out hatefully. Paul rolled his eyes in disgust. He'd grin and bear it, or so he thought.

The final straw came as Paul stepped into the shower. He stood there, freezing, with the hot water beating down on him.

<ring> <ring>

Oh, you have got to be kidding me, he thought as he realized the shower curtain was about a foot too short to go across the entire opening of the bathtub-shower combination. *Why is there this weird one-foot section of marble back here?*

<ring> <ring>

Playing with different placements of the curtain, Paul finally settled on something in the center, being careful to try to keep his body completely positioned under the water.

<ring> <ring>

<ring> <ring>

<ring> <ring>

"Good grief," he muttered as he washed the last bit of soap off and exited the shower. Wrapping a towel around himself, he scrambled for the phone to see who the incessant caller was.

"Hello?"

"Are you kidding me?" Nicole screamed from the other end.

"What?"

"I was just about to take a shower, and the damn shower curtain is too short!"

"I know…except I was already in the shower when I realized it," Paul said in his best sarcastic tone.

"Mmnt! Who does that? Really?"

"I don't know," Paul replied flatly. "But that's the first time my boys have gone from proud grapes to tiny raisins in a *hot* shower! The wind from the air-conditioner whipping around that curtain was quite vile." Perking up, he added, "Good luck with *your* shower, though. He-he."

"Oh, hell to the no. Trust and believe we are getting new rooms first thing in the morning. Meet me downstairs at seven-thirty."

"Sounds good. Night."

"Mmnt. Night."

Day Two: Monday

The next morning, Paul and Nicole approached the pleasant hotel minion together.

"How may I help you?" the girl minion asked.

"Hi, we checked in yesterday, and there are some slight problems with our rooms," Nicole said in her normal sunshiny voice.

[NICOLE'S NOTE: *You can catch more flies with honey, I always say.*]
[PAUL'S NOTE: *Except that day.*]

"Oh, I'm sorry, ma'am. What seems to be the problem?"

"Well, to start with," Paul cut in, "the carpet is frayed and thread-bare near the door of my room. In addition, my wallpaper is peeling. There are some mold spots in my bathroom, and my TV only gets one channel."

"And," Nicole added, "Our shower curtains don't go all the way across our showers. My junk was freezing last night in that shower!"

Everyone laughed, trying to make light of the situation. Deep down, though, Paul and Nicole were not amused with the girl minion's perky demeanor and the way her beady eyes squinted when she smiled, pretending to care about their plight.

"Well, I certainly apologize for the carpet, wallpaper, mold in your room, and TV, sir. We're in the middle of remodeling our rooms, and you're both in the tower that hasn't been remodeled yet."

Clouds start to move in on Nicole's sunshiny day.

"But, unfortunately, those bathtub-shower combinations are built that way with that little extra piece in the back so you can sit on it or put your leg up there for shaving."

"First," Nicole started, a neck roll imminent, "who would sit on that? It's marble, and being that it's a natural stone, it's cold! Second, if you were going to put it there, why didn't you buy shower curtains that went all the way across?"

"I don't know, ma'am. I'm sorry."

Neck roll number one.

"Well," Paul said, "how about the remodeled rooms in the other tower? Do they have the same setup?"

"No sir, but..."

Thunder.

"...those rooms are only for our *preferred* members. I'm sorry."

Lightning.

"Given the situation, can't we be upgraded to preferred status?" Paul hoped.

"I'm sorry, sir, but I can't do that." And, with that, the minion was downgraded to revolting troll.

"Do you at least have another room in our current tower that doesn't have jacked-up carpet and wallpaper?" Paul asked.

"I don't think so, but let me check, sir."

Rain.

"No, I'm sorry. Because it's the NBA All Star weekend, we're totally booked."

"Just so I'm clear, there is no possibility we can switch rooms in the four nights we're here, then?" Nicole pressed.

"No, ma'am. I'm sorry."

Neck roll number two.

Tornado.

"Fine. Thank you," Nicole said curtly, and she and Paul stormed off.

"Really?" Nicole grumbled once they were out of earshot. "Really?"

"That's why the conference isn't here, I'll bet," Paul added.

Not one to dwell on the negative, Nicole took pause. "You know what, it doesn't matter. We're barely going to be in our rooms. We are here to learn and have fun. Let's just get to the conference, grab a little breakfast, and get a good seat for the keynote speaker."

"You're right. Let's go. You know we have to walk, right?"

"Do you see any cute shoes on my feet today? No. You know that's not how I roll, but my little piggies have been to the sausage factory and need some time in a looser casing today."

The hotel hosting the conference was only two doors down, and they'd seen a people mover the day before when they registered, so they knew once they made it those two blocks, everything would be fine. They would just step on it and ride it all the way in.

Approaching the conference hotel, though, their hopes of an easy ride vanished. The people mover taking people into the conference was broken. It was working fine taking people in the other direction, but that was not the direction they needed.

"Can't a sister just get a break?" Nicole said, disappointed. "Really?"

"Let's just get there," Paul chuckled. "First the room, then your poor feet, and now this. It's almost funny."

"And yet it's not," Nicole replied, stepping off the nonmoving people mover and beginning the last part of their walk into the hotel.

As they entered the hotel, signs said the conference was downstairs. They headed toward the escalator and, when Paul stepped on it to head down, it stopped. Afraid he'd broken it, he jumped back off.

"Oh my God! Did the escalator just break?" Paul screeched, looking over at Nicole, eyes wide in horror. Everyone else already on the escalator turned to look at him. Paul flushed. "I didn't do anything. Promise! I just stepped on it. No, I really just hovered my foot over it. I'm so sorry," he called out.

With his mouth now in a permanent O shape, Paul stared at the escalator, trying to will it to start back up.

Nicole, having had an unusual few moments of silence, finally said, "Unbelievable. Truly, Paul, you've outdone yourself."

"What? I didn't break it! I'm not *that* fat!"

"So, let's recap. Our hotel rooms have issues, our feet are broke down, I rode the tram last night in my bare feet and probably caught God knows what, we can't switch rooms, the people movers are broken—"

"Well," Paul interrupted, "just the one people mover coming into the hotel."

"Right," she continued. "The people mover *we* needed coming into the hotel is broken, and now the escalator that could have easily taken us down to our conference broke when you put your little pinky toe on it. Does that cover it?"

"Pretty much."

"Really?" she said, emphasizing it with a little head tilt.

"I know. Let's find the stairs."

Thankfully, the first day of the conference went without incident. Having enjoyed themselves and snapped up lots of cool swag for their teams from the vendors, they picked another buffet to attack and discussed their battle plan.

As they left the conference hotel, reality kicked them in the bellies again. This time, the people mover leaving the hotel was broken and the one coming into the hotel was working.

[PAUL'S NOTE: *People, you just can't make this stuff up. It really happened. Really.*]

"It's broken, isn't it?" Paul said rhetorically.

"Yes, yes it is," Nicole replied, shaking her head in disbelief.

"What else, Nic? What else could go wrong? How have three things broken when we've tried to get on them today? Who does that happen to? Really?" Paul tilted his head sideways, mimicking Nicole's movement from earlier that morning.

"You know what? It's fine," Nicole said, smiling. "We were sitting all day in those seminars. We can make it two blocks to the buffet, and then we're going to embrace our bigness and be knee-deep in all that seafood again. After that, it's Cirque du Soleil, which is going to be amazing, so pick your hooves up and let's go!"

Shaking all over like a dog trying to rid himself of the bad mojo, Paul found the strength to smile, and they continued on. About a block down, Nicole piped up. "Wait, wait, wait. My feet are killing me again. I need to stop for a minute."

"We've only been a block. I thought it was fine because we'd been sitting in all those seminars," Paul said mockingly.

"I know what I said. You don't have to repeat it. Why do you have to take such long strides?"

"Because I'm six four and have long legs. You know long strides burn more calories. We're never going to get anywhere, though, with your feet in this condition, and we've still got three more days."

"Just focus on the food and the show," Nicole repeated to herself as she began to slowly move again.

When they arrived at the buffet, they braced for the trumpets, choir, and angels again. As they surveyed their options, one food group was very conspicuously missing.

"Excuse me," Nicole said, soliciting the nearest hotel minion.

"Where is the seafood? I don't see it."

"I'm sorry, ma'am. The seafood buffet is only on the weekends. Today's Monday, so we don't have it."

"Really? That is so disappointing," she said, frowning, clearly irritated that the minion felt it important to point out what day of the week it was to her.

"How about some fish, ma'am?" the boy minion asked politely. "We do have that."

"That is not the same, and don't pretend you can substitute shrimp and crabs with a little nasty piece of fried catfish," Nicole briskly told him.

[PAUL'S NOTE: *It was obvious to me at this point, just like the girl minion from earlier in the day, that he had been downgraded to revolting troll as well, and I knew what was coming next because I could see it in Nicole's face. His best exit strategy was to just leave but, unfortunately, he was a persistent little troll.*]

"Oh no, we have several types, both grilled and fried," he replied proudly, holding his ground.

"Didn't I just say I didn't want fish?"

"Perhaps something else grilled then?"

"Boy, I just walked two blocks on the Strip with feet that are to' up from the flo' up, and you just told me you don't have a seafood buffet, which is all I wanted after the unbelievably bad day I've had. Now I've got to settle for sloppy seconds and select something else. I'll tell you once to back up and retreat from my sight. I am D-O-N-E."

"Yes, ma'am." And with that, the troll cast her one final glance over his shoulder and quickly disappeared. Nicole felt sure he went back to his bridge to guard it.

"The desserts are still pretty good," Paul said when Nicole finally returned to their table with a barely filled plate of food.

"Shut up. I want king crab. Lots and lots of king crab legs. Instead, I have a pauper's plate full of crappy ass wings."

"This is not like you. You are always so full of sunshine. Let's do what you said earlier and just focus on the show we have coming up in an hour. We don't have to walk far to get there, and we have great seats."

"Mmnt. Okay."

After dinner, the walk was indeed not far to the theater, and they enjoyed themselves. Walking back to their rooms, their spirits were lifted, and they each lumbered off to their "non-preferred" lowly rooms.

Day Three: Tuesday

Three good things happened on day three. First, their boss took them to dinner, along with seven other colleagues, at a fancy seafood restaurant. As everyone was being seated, two "seafood tower" appetizers appeared; Nicole *finally* got her fill of crab legs.

The second good thing was the comedy show they saw. It was a hypnotist show, and it had them ROFLWMM and LMAOPIMP. It was great.

The very best thing that happened to them, however, happened at the end of the night after the comedy show. Famished from laughing so hard, Paul and Nicole had a taste for something sweet.

[PAUL'S NOTE: *Well, I had a taste for something sweet, and Nicole is very easy to convince.*]

They stopped at one of the numerous twenty-four hour restaurants in one of the hotels and ordered dessert. Nicole ordered a German Chocolate brownie and, after she took the first bite, you'd have thought that brownie descended from heaven itself the way she slapped the table, threw her head back in the air, and started speaking in tongues. She caressed every bite of that brownie like it was a young, nubile lover, and when it was gone she shed a single tear because she knew it would never be as good as that first time.

[NICOLE'S NOTE: *Sing it with me, y'all. I'm talking about Sade's "Never as Good as the First Time."*]

Returning to their hotel in a state of blind euphoria from the German Chocolate brownie, neither of them minded the ghetto so much. They even planned on hitting the slot machines the following night. Little did they know that fate wasn't done with Paul yet, and the next morning she played her final hand.

Day Four: Wednesday
<ring> <ring>
　　<ring> <ring>
　　"Hello? Did my alarm not go off? Am I late?" Paul stammered, trying to wake up and figure out what was going on, assuming he was late for their last day of seminars.
　　"I don't know. How late were you out last night?" said the irritated voice on the other end.
　　"Marilyn?"
　　"I thought when you called me at eleven thirty last night, you were going to bed!"

"Marilyn?" he asked again, still wiping the sleep from his eyes.

"Are you that tired? Really? Yes, it's me. Answer the question."

"What are you talking about? I did go to bed after we talked," Paul said defensively, finally hearing the aggravation in his wife's voice.

"Then what did you do last night?"

"I told you. We went to dinner with our boss, went to a comedy show, and then went for a late-night snack."

"What else?"

"There is nothing else! What is going on? It's too early for your female mind games, so just tell me already."

Momentary silence.

"There is $2,500 in charges in our checking account this morning," she responded, clearly annoyed with Paul's last comment.

"What? From where?"

"Some place named Domain something or other. So, did you buy everyone in the whole damn bar a drink, or did you lose all that money gambling?"

Now irritated, Paul shot back, "First of all, I brought two rolls of quarters with me to gamble with, and I haven't even used them yet because we've had such lousy luck out here. Second, when have you ever seen me have more than one or two drinks anywhere? Third, what is the actual name of the places the charges are from?"

"Need some time to come up with a story, do you?"

"What? No, of course not!"

"Are you in some kind of trouble? Is someone there with you now and you can't tell me?" her voice becoming very high-pitched and frantic now.

"Are you serious? Really?"

"Just say 'Mondo' if you're in trouble. I'll understand," she said, quickly lowering her voice and speaking in a whisper.

"Oh my God, have *you* been drinking? Just tell me again where the charges are from! I'm sitting here in my boxers and a t-shirt, *alone*, trying to figure out what the hell is going on!"

"Mmnt. One minute." After a couple of seconds, she said, "It says, 'Domain Solutions'."

"Anything else?" Paul asked.

"Yes, it does say 'autorenew' in the description…" She hesitated, now obviously realizing it couldn't have been a bar or casino.

"Wow, that's not good," Paul said, exhausted all of a sudden. "That's the company I order domains from for my job. The last time I ordered one, I only had our check card on me, so I bought the domain with that. They must have kept it on file and then auto-renewed a butt-load of domains with it. Unbelievable."

"What's a domain?"

"You know, it's the words that come after the www in the address bar of your Internet browser, and they usually end in dot com or dot net. We buy a bunch of those related to our products so other companies can't."

"Well, the only domain we're going to be in is the welfare domain if you don't get this straightened out," Marilyn remarked.

"Yeah, I know. Okay, I'm sorry. Let me make some calls, hon. I'll let you know. Bye."

<ring> <ring>

<ring> <ring>

"Hello? Am I late? Did my alarm not go off?"

"Oh my God! It's back!"

"What?" came Nicole's sleepy voice.

"The bad luck! You'll never believe what's happened now."

Sitting up and preparing for the rest, Nicole took a deep breath and said, "Okay. Tell me."

Paul recounted the story quickly and asked her to take notes at the first seminar so he could stay and try to get the charges reversed. All Nicole could respond with was, "Really?"

In the end, the charges did not get reversed, but Paul's company cut him a check very quickly and helped him avoid the welfare lines.

Day Five: Thursday

Grateful their insufferable week in Vegas was finally over, Paul and Nicole made a final trek through the ghetto to check out. Afterward, while curbside waiting for the next taxi, Paul noticed that Nicole was fidgety.

"Are you okay?" Paul asked.

"Yeah, I guess."

"Are you feeling okay? Is it your feet?"

"Yeah, I feel fine. My feet aren't fine, but they're recovering."

"So what is it?"

"Nothing really."

"Just tell me. At this point, nothing will surprise me."

"It's really stupid, but I want to get another German Chocolate brownie before we go."

Instant laughter. "Are you kidding? Hahaahaaa! You are so funny!"

"I can't help it. It's all I've thought about for the last two days," she said guiltily. "It's the only good thing about this trip. Do we have time?"

"No, and even if we did, something would happen on the way there. You'd trip and fall or I'd lose my wallet or something. We need to just pray we make it to the airport and back home in one piece. This has been the worst week."

"I know you're right, but I *really* want it," she pleaded. "Do you think they can ship it?"

"Really? Welcome to the dark side of dessert, my friend. I'm sure we'll be back again someday."

"Mmnt."

When Paul and Nicole returned to work, they shared their tale of misery and woe to anyone who would listen. Hysteria often ensued at their expense, but out of the darkness came one bright spot. The word "Really?" took on a whole new meaning, and it quickly became the companion phrase to "Mmnt!" You couldn't hear one without the other:

"Eww, your child vomited on you last night? Oh, and a little went in your mouth!? Mmnt! Really? Why did you even come to work today? You are probably contagious!" (And then Mondo! your way out of that conversation!)

"That heffa is using a handicap hang tag, and she isn't even pregnant or limping? Mmnt! Really?" (And don't forget the very appropriate neck roll with this one.)

Invoking your BS Degree

When you've smoked out the hot mess from a mile away, it's time to invoke your BS (bullshit) degree with a simple, condescending "Really?" Here of some proper examples of when "Really?" should be used:

1. The printer breaks down when you're trying to print copies for a meeting you're already late to. Really?
2. People who had previously accepted an invite to a potluck decide at the last minute not to participate, but still slide through the line to make a plate. Really?

    [NICOLE'S NOTE: *FYI, the appropriate thing to do in this situation is to just quietly bring the potluck coordinator an expensive gift or bauble so she'll forget about how your greedy ass messed up her potluck matrix, okay?*]

3. You're a salaried employee who has worked numerous weekends and nights, and you get into work thirty minutes late one day. As you're leaving at five o'clock, your boss stops you and asks what time you got in so he can appropriately count it toward your vacation time. Really?

4. The resource hog just got promoted from peon to director… and everyone knows the position only opened up after she opened up! Really?

Trimming the Fat

Turn negatives into positives. Remember, no matter how bad things seem, it could be worse, so look for the fun and use it as a way to bring out the good (even if it's a just a good laugh at how horrible things seem). It's easier than you think, and it will help keep your spirits uplifted and your funny bone intact.

D-O-N-E

When you have had enough of something or someone and can't take one more second of it, you are D-O-N-E. Done like, "Stick a fork in me, I'm done."

Heart of the Story

Paul done come up with this one, too. "Done come up." Get it?

As with Mmnt!, the pronunciation of D-O-N-E is most important. First, you say, "I am *done!*" really emphasizing the word "done" as you conclude the sentence. Then, for added drama, you have to spell it out. D-O-N-E. Then, you finish with another "Done." When you put it all together, it goes like this: "I am done! D-O-N-E! Done!"

Think of a situation you are sick and tired of dealing with. Maybe your partner has been boinking off the reservation (i.e. cheating on you) and for some stupid reason you've stuck by the cheater instead of bleeding him or her dry for every penny his or her sorry ass is worth. Maybe you're the type of person who can walk by a bakery, inhale the heavenly scent of baking bread or fresh-baked cookies, and instantly gain five pounds. It doesn't matter. Just think of something you need a release from, and repeat after us: "I am *done!* D-O-N-E! Done!" Say it again! "D-O-N-E!" There, don't you feel better? We do.

 Tail

Normally, when you think of the pitter-patter of little feet, you think about a child's footsteps, all tiny and small and sweet and innocent, right? Paul and Nicole did, too…until they started working at one of their companies together. Mmnt!

When Paul and Nicole arrived for their first day on the job, they were escorted to a nice secluded area of cubes near the cafeteria.

[NICOLE'S NOTE: *Yes, we were Hooves Highing ourselves for being lucky enough to be steps away from the food. Later, after the incident, not so much.*]

The cubes had been lived in before, but things were clean, set up, and awaiting their arrival. They were told their cube locations were temporary until a new seating arrangement was finalized and that they shouldn't get too comfortable.

This was a hard rule for Paul and Nicole to abide by. Paul had lots of toys, like squishy balls, Nerf guns, and Potato Heads that needed displaying, along with several inspirational posters, like "Come to the dark side. We have cookies," or "A balanced diet is a cookie in each hand." Nicole, on the other hand, liked to incorporate knick-knacks, tchotchkes, pictures, and plants.

[PAUL'S NOTE: *And let me tell you, she has this organizer she keeps her lotions in, which is fine on its own, but she put this tired-looking foliage in there to hide the lotions that is just hideous. When I say tired foliage, I mean* tired. *The leaves are so faded from the sun that they've gone from green to brown like a real dead plant. Mmnt!*]
[NICOLE'S NOTE: *You need to watch it! My mama made me that organizer and planted that fake foliage for me. If she reads this, she is gonna knock you into next week! Mmnt!*]

Anyway, asking Paul and Nicole to not get comfortable is like telling Santa Claus not to come on Christmas Eve. Regardless, trying to be accommodating in their new surroundings, they each left about four boxes of cube clutter in their car trunks. As a result, one whole set of drawers in Paul's desk remained empty.

About three weeks after settling in, Paul noticed a foul smell in the air. It didn't linger, so he assumed it was just someone walking by with offensive body odor (and he made a mental note to find out who the culprit was later).

The next day, he smelled something again. This time, assuming some idiot had burned something in the microwave in the cafeteria the night before and the noxious odor was just finally making its way to their area, he tried to ignore it.

On the third day, the smell returned but was a bit more pungent. Sitting in his chair and turning from right to left, he noticed it seemed to be stronger on the right. Wondering if maybe the smell was him, he casually began sniffing himself, hoping to God it wasn't some orifice he'd forgotten to deodorize.

[PAUL'S NOTE: *In case you've never performed the casual sniffing maneuver, let me explain. There are four places you need to check: your hair, your armpits, your crotch, and your feet. If you're a guy, smelling your hair is probably hard to do. If you haven't washed it in a couple of days, though, it very well may be the culprit. For girls, you can usually bring a piece of hair from around the side, and in a move that looks like you're restyling your hair, quickly smell a strand or two and decide. For your armpits, stretch your arm out on your desk and then lean your head under your desk like you dropped something and are looking for it. As you're going down, inhale. If you fall out of your seat from the stench, you've found the guilty party. Your crotch is tricky, but there's an easy one-two move you can implement that will allow you to check both your crotch and your feet at the same time. While sitting in a chair, simply spread your legs apart a little and bend down at the center to tie your shoe. As you bend, draw in air from your crotch, and when you get lower toward your feet, draw in again. If it's one of those two areas, run, don't walk, to the nearest drugstore and freshen that mess up. Mmnt!*]

After sniffing all appropriate areas and feeling assured it wasn't himself, Paul started looking around. First, he checked out his desk for potential hidden food that may have spoiled. Nothing. Next, he looked in the set of drawers he'd placed papers and folders in, in case there was some errant food he'd forgotten about. Nothing. He got up and looked around the perimeter of his cube, thinking maybe something had fallen on the floor and started to reek. Still nothing. He casually perused his neighbors' cubes, convinced now it must be them with the distasteful smell. Nothing again. Confused, Paul sat back down, and when he did, the smell definitely seemed more odorous. Finally, in a last-ditch effort, he began opening his empty set of drawers. In the bottom drawer, he got his answer. There rested a family of dead mice, turned sideways, claws in the air, eyes still open. With the lethal smell now pouring out of the drawer, Paul cried, "I am done! D-O-N-E! Done!"

Having heard that expression before, Nicole jumped into action. "What's wrong?"

"You won't believe it. Come here!"

Rushing over, Nicole was instantly attacked by both the stench and the sight of the dead mice family. "Oh my God! Are they dead?"

"Yes, look at their little paws. They're sideways in the air like they were doing the Thriller dance and then just keeled over. I've smelled something funny for the last couple of days, but I just kept assuming it was something or someone else. This is disgusting."

Having drawn a crowd now, Paul told and retold the story over and over. Never one to miss an opportunity to be in the spotlight,

Nicole provided her best grimacing face to the crowd during appropriate story moments. She even threw in an "I can't believe it" and a "Wow!" here and there so the attention was never fully on Paul and his angst.

[PAUL'S NOTE: *And, you know, that is so typical of you. Always trying to hog my moment.*]
[NICOLE'S NOTE: *Really? What moment? People were concerned there might be more mice running around in* their *drawers. They didn't care about your shock and awe.*]
[PAUL'S NOTE: *That's not true! People were genuinely concerned about my mice infestation!*]
[NICOLE'S NOTE: *Very nice.*]

Once everyone was fully briefed on what had transpired, HR and Facilities were called to assess the situation and lay the poor little Michael Jackson mice to rest. As a result of the dead mice family, though, everyone in the building was put on eating restrictions. All personal food stashes were to be taken home that night, and everyone had to begin eating in the cafeteria.

The new rules caused quite the uproar. People loved eating at their desks, and being forced to go the cafeteria while the mice problem was being eradicated did not sit well with them. Paul and Nicole heard people announcing they needed a breath mint, getting up and leaving their desk, and then not returning for fifteen minutes until it had fully dissolved. Productivity slowed tremendously because, instead of noshing on a bagel during the morning meeting, people would have to pit stop in the cafeteria to get their carb fix.

[NICOLE'S NOTE: *Secretly, I think the nonsmokers loved it because they were using this as their way to get back at all their smoker friends who took smoke breaks every hour. LOL!*]

Two months later, HR provided the all-clear sign, allowing everyone to eat at their desks again. By then, Paul and Nicole had moved to their new cubes (nowhere near the cafeteria, much to their dismay) and had happily decorated them to the hilt.

[PAUL'S NOTE: *Even that ugly, tired foliage came back. Mmnt!*]
[NICOLE'S NOTE: *Yes, it did, because my mama made it. I already told you that! Our cubes really were the standard against which everyone else was judged, though. We decorated by season, and people were always parading by to see what we'd done.*]
[PAUL'S NOTE: *There you go again. Attention whore.*]

In the fall of that year, like a bad sequel to a horror movie, the mice family returned. Well, not the dead ones because those would be zombie mice and everyone knows that would be ridiculous. We can only assume they were extended family members of the deceased.

It was about 10:00 a.m. on Tuesday and time for Paul's morning snack. He kept a constant supply of cherry granola bars (they are like a small piece of cherry pie heaven) and one-hundred-calorie snack packs in his desk for just such occasions. As he opened his bottom drawer, he was visually violated by a huge mouse nest made of empty granola bar wrappers and snack-pack boxes. Just the day before, that drawer had been beautifully lined with uneaten snacks and, in the course of twenty-four hours, it had been demolished and turned into a mouse love den.

Afraid to touch it, Paul yelled for help, knowing some minion would come trotting along, willing to venture into his rodent den of iniquity. That one such minion was his boss, who happily reached in, grabbed the nest with both hands, and dumped it into Paul's trash.

Once the fear of encountering a live mouse was out of the way, Paul finished the job by taking the drawer out, throwing everything away, and disinfecting the hell out of it. He returned the empty drawer to its place and instant messaged Nicole.

"OMG! THEY'RE BACK!" Paul typed.

"Who?" Nicole responded.

"THEM!"

"Them who?"

"The mice."

Silence. Waiting. Blinking cursor.

"What are you talking about! The mice are back?" came a shriek from behind Paul's back.

Jumping, Paul said, "Oh my God, you scared me. They *are* back! They made a love nest out of my granola bars." With that, he pointed to his trash. Nicole peered inside and saw the remains.

"Did you see them?" she asked, looking around the floor for any evidence of movement.

"No, but yesterday, they weren't here. My drawer was fine. They ate that whole box in one night. I can't believe it. The mice community blames me for that mice family's demise a few months back, and now they've returned to claim their revenge!"

"Uh-huh. Well, now that there's no food for them to eat, I'm sure they'll leave you alone. Speaking of leaving, I'm gone, too. I don't want them eyeballing me and following me back to my desk. See ya."

Paul returned to his work. About an hour later, he heard a faint scratching sound. He stopped, turned around, and looked at the drawer, waiting to hear it again. Nothing. Turning back around, Paul continued typing. More scratching. Paul turned again and stared at the drawer. Nothing. Hesitantly, he reached his hand out and gently eased open the edge of the drawer. In a burst of motion, three mice jumped out and scurried around the side of his cube.

"AHHHH!" Paul screamed before he could stop himself, and he threw his hands over his mouth to try to stifle it. He called Nicole on the phone. "I am done! D-O-N-E! Done! Get over here. They are still taunting me!"

Running over, Nicole asked, "Now what?"

"They were scratching inside the drawer, and when I opened it, three of them jumped out and ran off!"

"Oh my God!!" she screamed and jumped on the nearest chair. "Where did they go?"

"Toward Tina."

"Quick. Mondo! her."

Paul whipped around and typed the secret Mondo! word into his instant message window with Tina.

"Who?" Tina quickly responded back. "I can see you both at your cube, but no one else is there."

"It's not a *who*. It's a what," Paul typed back.

Swiftly, Tina got up and marched over. "What are you talking about? The rules of Mondo! clearly state you can only use it when you need rescuing from someone. Last time you called me over, it was because you needed to use Mondo! retrospectively. That was a one-time exception. I won't allow it again."

"Well, this is somewhat retrospectively," Paul said hesitantly, "but the situation is different. There is another mice infestation, and they just jumped out of my drawer and were headed straight for you!"

"What?" Tina squealed. "Are you kidding me?"

"No," Nicole said, and she proceeded to narrate the entire story for Tina as if she'd been there and lived through the horror herself.

"I'm so sorry," Tina said, repulsed.

"Thank you," Nicole answered in her most sincere voice.

"Bitch, I am the one she's talking to!" Paul quipped, cocking his head to the side and giving her the skunk eye. "Why are you thanking her? You weren't even here! Mmnt! Always with the drama and the spotlight stealing. Go get your own mice. Now, Tina, like you were saying...."

"I know you're not talking to me!" Nicole exclaimed, and she began doing neck rolls like she was a broken record.

"I was talking to you, so step off," Paul said, glaring. Then he refocused on Tina. "Tina, please continue with your pity. It's helping me through this rough time."

"You two are both drama whores. I was just saying 'I'm sorry'. However, if those little vermin come to visit me, I will stomp their asses into the ground. I suppose I'll allow nonhuman Mondos as well. Carry on!" Tina returned to her kingdom, looking down at the floor as she walked and scrutinizing her every step.

[PAUL'S NOTE: *She was probably afraid she was going to fall again and have gay neck! Ha!*]

By now, everyone had heard the commotion, and they came over in droves. Paul told the story, demonstrated the mice's exit strategy, and warned everyone living in that direction that they were on the move. People instantly began looking for signs of invasion in their own desks or offices. One coworker found a huge nest in her overhead storage cabinet as well as a hole that had been chewed through her cube wall. It was obvious then what had been going on. They were living in the penthouse in her overhead cabinet at night and dining at Paul's restaurant by day, where the treats were both bite-sized and filling.

"I can't believe they came back to check my drawer," Paul told Nicole a little later after things died down. "I bleached that drawer out. Surely they could smell that."

"Maybe you threw away their babies," she said evenly, trying to conceal a smile.

"Don't tease like that," Paul said, quickly kicking his trashcan a couple of times, looking for movement. "Where do they hide? When I took the drawer out, I looked behind there. There was nothing. It was clean. I can't even figure out how they got in there," he continued.

"You just didn't look hard enough. I bet they were there, all *Mission Impossible*-like, with their tiny little paws and backs plastered up against the back of the drawer, trying to escape your stare. Obviously, it worked." Nicole laughed.

"Those beady-eyed little bastards better not have done that."

"Just watch," and in a moment of defiance, Nicole jerked the drawer open. To her horror, one of the perpetrators had returned to the scene of the crime. *"Ahhhhh!!"* she screamed, jumping back a good five yards.

Tina came running back over again. "What now?"

"I opened Paul's drawer and one of them was in there! I was trying to be funny and make a point, but I didn't expect one to really be there!" Nicole continued to shriek.

"Which way did he go?"

"Back toward your desk like last time," Paul interjected, slamming the drawer back into place. "Now do you both feel my pain? It's just too much."

"I am done. D-O-N-E. Done!" Nicole protested, and she marched over to their boss's office to see what kind of work-from-home schedule she could negotiate until the mice were gone.

"Tina, I've been violated. Why do the mice keep targeting me? I never leave any open containers or food out," Paul moaned.

"I don't know, honey, but they've got you in their sights now, and it looks like they're not going to stop until they break you. Just stay strong."

"Mmnt. I am done!"

And, with that, everyone endured another food quarantine for a second round of mice extermination. Paul exited the company before they could return a third time.

[PAUL'S NOTE: *Because homey don't play that.*]
[NICOLE'S NOTE: *What are you talking about? You left for a great job opportunity!*]

[PAUL'S NOTE: *I was still done and considering leaving. The mice were traumatizing.*]
[NICOLE'S NOTE: *Very nice.*]

Trimming the Fat

Find a humorous and non-confrontational way to let others know when you've reached your limit. Keeping the air light will help keep the conversation flowing, and you'll stand a better chance of getting your way. Tread carefully, though, because this tactic can quickly lose effect if used too often, and you'll begin to sound more like a whiner than just a frustrated hoofer.

The Phisher

Meaning

Office gossips who present themselves as being factual and established when they are really presenting you a virtual reality and simply fishing for anything to make their story more enticing for someone to bite…hook, line, and sinker.

Heart of the Story

Nicole made this one up on the fly during a heated exchange in the story you're about to read.

Phishers are always trying to lure and capture the meatiest stories. They know how to take a two-pound fish, stretch it into a twenty-pound whopper, gut it, cook it, and feed it to the hungry masses. The problem is that when confronted, they often backpedal, offering someone else up on the platter. You know, the "Well that's what so-and-so told me!" or the "That's what I was told!" excuse. Either way, phishers love to dish it, but they certainly cannot take it and are often unable to produce facts.

We must admit, though, that phishers can have the most tantalizing stories. They're usually quite juicy and filled with all sorts of drama and smut. Phisher stories leave you *ooohing* and *ahhing* and wishing you had been there to see it all unfold.

Just be careful, though. When phishers are fishing, they're not only telling you the juice, but their radar is also up, and everything you say is on the record. *"Anything you say to a phisher can and will be used against you in the court of gossip."* Remember to mind your Ps and Qs and to simply keep your ears open and your mouth shut. Otherwise, it will be your tantalizing story on the dinner plate!

Tail

There's nothing like a good office party, especially when the company provides all the food and spirits! There's also nothing like all the stories people walk away with at the end of the night because something always happens that starts tongues wagging the next day. Someone gets wasted and tells company secrets, an office resource hog gets exposed for offering horizontal refreshments (if you know what we mean), or a situation gets blown out of proportion and retold with such excess and exaggeration that it sounds nothing like what really happened. One company Paul and Nicole worked for was no different. It hosted quarterly happy hours to give its IT teams an opportunity to unwind and mix and mingle with each other after hours.

Nicole's first week on the job just so happened to be the same week as one such function. Paul realized very quickly that Nicole was a social butterfly. That, coupled with the fact that during his interview with her she hadn't related his famous name and attractive head of hair to the hair-care guy but rather to the only US importer of Patrón tequila, prompted Paul to keep close tabs on Nicole at her debut after-hours office function. After a couple of hours, he was exhausted from trying to keep up with his new manager who was flitting from one table to another, rounding out her second margarita and looking for her third. Yes, while everyone else was just getting started, Nicole was being walked out by her overly protective "parent" at 8:30 p.m.!

[NICOLE'S NOTE: *For the record, I am not a lush, and I can hold my liquor very well. I was the best bartender at my restaurant back in the day.*]
[PAUL'S NOTE: *Very nice.*]

Of course, wild rumors came back the next day, and Nicole was furious she'd missed the episodes behind them. Jon, our Creole co-worker who lived up to the expectations of a Louisiana Creole boy, got hit on all night by the Silver Fox. The Silver Fox was a petite, sassy, and very hip sixty-something-year-old who had a wide-on for Jon, who was thirty-something and happily married. In addition, Sandy was spotted by several people hopping on top of the bar and saying, "Hey, whoever wants a buttery nipple or Girl Scout, get over here!" Sandy was talking about a round of buttery nipple and Girl Scout shots but, by the time Nicole heard it, Sandy was a naughty Girl Scout exposing her ta-tas and rubbing butter on them for all the boys to try. Nicole was in a tizzy and upset she'd missed it all, and was on pins and needles waiting for the next team get-together.

[PAUL'S NOTE: *For those of you not in the know, a wide-on is the female equivalent of a hard-on for men.*]

Have you ever heard the saying, "Be careful what you wish for"? How about, "Karma's a bitch"? Well, Nicole got them both at the Christmas party a few months later.

By the time the Christmas party rolled around, Nicole knew damn near all of IT and many people within the corporate office. She was Norm from *Cheers*. When she walked in the room, it was like a cheer...*Nicole*! And boy, did she love it!

[PAUL'S NOTE: *Attention whore.*]

She schmoozed her way around the room in the direction of the bar to obtain a Texas margarita, adding "Two, please" behind her order. After all, the lines were long and her shoes were cute. There wasn't going to be any unnecessary waiting in line tonight.

Drinks in hand, she made her way to the buffet. That was her first clue the night might be going horribly wrong. There was no buffet, just two food stations: one offering roasted lunch meat with rolls, and the other roasted veggies, fruit, and desserts.

"Where's the food?" Nicole spat out.

A resounding *"I know!"* came back from the herd in front of her.

This just was not going to do. Nicole had her mind all made up that tonight was *the* night for craziness, and with the piss-poor finger foods and plate of nothingness she'd assembled, no one was going to hang around long enough to get into any trouble.

[PAUL'S NOTE: *Well, we did see one crazy thing. Remember Santa's pimp?*]

[NICOLE'S NOTE: *<gasp> Oh my God! Men, I support those of you who get into the spirit of Christmas. I really do. After all, it's usually us girls who wear our Santa sweatshirts, Christmas earrings, etc. However, it is not cool to wear an all-red suit, a green shirt, green tie, red gators, and a red top hat with a green sash around it. All he was missing was a pimp cup and his ho, ho, hos!*]

While back in line a little later for another Texas 'rita, she heard several people talking about an after party. Nicole quickly snagged an invite. After another hour, everyone left and made their way to…

[PAUL'S NOTE: *Those three little dots are code for "Nicole can't remember because she was so to' up from the flo' up"!*]

[NICOLE'S NOTE: *I plead the Fifth.*]

[PAUL'S NOTE: *Very nice.*]

When they got to the after party, Harry bought a round. Then someone else bought a round. Food came to the table; people were laughing and joking around. New people joined the fun, and before they knew it, it was midnight and people were slowly leaving.

Nicole, one of the last faithful few to leave, was feeling no pain as she reached in her purse for her keys and started walking out. Ava, Salil, and Harry were in tow.

"Are you sure you're okay to drive?" Salil asked.

"Sure. I'm fine!" Nicole responded as she wobbled over to her car.

"Ummm, I'm not so sure," Ava rebutted, waving Harry over to help.

"Nicole, sweetie, why don't you let one of us drive you home?" Harry said as he reached over to take Nicole's keys.

"Well, if you insist," she said as she reluctantly handed her keys to Salil and told him the way.

[NICOLE'S NOTE: *Friends don't let friends drive drunk! I don't care who you are! I will say that while I typically hold my liquor very well, I was way out of my element that night and am* so *thankful to Ava, Harry, and Salil for driving me home. I love you guys! Thank you for making me do the right thing!*]

The next day when Paul arrived to work, a crowd was hovering near his door.

"Morning, peeps," Paul said cheerily.

"We need to talk," came a somber reply.

"Uh, okay. Come on in," Paul offered. The door shut behind them. "Is it that serious?" Paul asked, beginning to get concerned.

"It's about Nicole," they replied.

"What about Nic? Is she okay?"

"Yes and no."

"Yes and no! What does that mean? Is she hurt?" Paul asked with a sense of foreboding.

"No, no, she's fine in that sense."

"Okay, then in what sense is she not fine?"

"Well, you know we care about her and only want the best for her, so that's why we've come to you today. She's our boss, so we don't want to get in any trouble."

"Out with it," Paul demanded, clearly anxious now.

"Last night was bad. B-A-D. We heard about things she did at the after party that she should only be doing in the privacy of her own home."

"Wait. Back the train up. There was an after party and I wasn't invited?" Paul said, neck roll and all.

"Umm, yeah, but from what we heard, it wasn't your scene, white bread," came their sassy reply.

"Mmnt. Okay, just tell me what Nicole did and how much damage control I'm going to have to do," Paul said, making a mental note to investigate where the after party was and why he was left out.

"Well," they began feebly, "we thought it was funny when they told us about Nicole getting on the table to dance, and we laughed when we heard the part about her singing into the light fixture and pretending to shimmy her shirt up, but then when they said she really did lift it up—"

"And she didn't have a bra—" someone interrupted in a quick whisper.

"We started to get concerned," the storyteller continued, getting a little more animated now.

"Nicole was free-birding it? That can't be true," Paul murmured.

"But the worst part was when she started talking about wanting to give our CIO a lap dance in her red Santa thong—"

"And that she didn't care that either of them were married—" the whisperer interjected.

"*Do what?*" Paul stammered. "She wanted to give our CIO a lap dance?"

"In her red Santa thong," the whisperer repeated.

"Here's the worst part."

"Wait. There's more?" Paul sighed, grabbing the side of his chair and bracing for impact.

"We think Nicole may have a drinking problem…." she paused, looking around for consensus from the team. After a couple of nods, she continued, "This isn't the first time we've heard her talk about drinking. She's told us about some of her escapades with her girls and getting her drink on. And now, with her getting drunk like this, we just feel like maybe it's habitual for her. We're afraid she's progressing into an alkie, and it's going to start affecting her work."

"Really?" came Paul's dumbfounded response.

"Really," they responded, almost in unison.

"Okay, well, I'll talk to her when she comes in. Thanks for coming and telling me…I guess," Paul said wearily.

After they left the room, Paul's heart was heavy. His worst fears had come to light. He and his team had been publicly embarrassed by one of his managers, and the person he thought was just a bubbly, fun-loving spirit was really a closet alcoholic skank-ass ho.

[NICOLE'S NOTE: *Okay, now it's time for me to hijack your story. It was not* that *bad, and I know you didn't really think that about me!*]
[PAUL'S NOTE: *You just don't know how convincing they were! I'd never had any alkie alliances or been part of an intervention before but, in my mind, I was trying to figure out how to stage one at work that would save both your face and mine. My load was heavy when I heard you unlock your office door that morning.*]

A soon as Paul heard Nicole's key in her office door, he jumped into action.

"Nic, we need to talk. Can you pop over?"

"Sure! Be right there," came her singsong voice. Paul thought he heard slurring.

[NICOLE'S NOTE: *Okay, now. Really?*]
[PAUL'S NOTE: *I'm telling you, I was a wreck. I really thought you were slurring your words. Then, in the thirty seconds it took you to walk to my office, my mind was racing with ideas on how I was going to have to sneak you out or keep you locked in your office all day so no one else saw. Then I started wondering how long you were going to be out while you "dried out" and how hard it was going to be to cover your job and mine, and then I thought about—oh, it was just horrible.*]
[NICOLE'S NOTE: *All that in thirty seconds?*]
[PAUL'S NOTE: *Yes, the mind is a powerful engine…if you're not drunk and slurring your words.*]
[NICOLE'S NOTE: *Okay, can we just get to the end of the story where I'm fully exonerated and cleared of these charges? People are really going to think I'm a lush ho.*]

"What's up?" Nicole asked.

"Please close the door and sit down. We need to talk," Paul responded seriously.

"Am I in trouble?" Nicole asked as she sat down.

"Well, your team came to me with some concerns this morning. It was about your behavior last night."

"Excuse me? My behavior?" Nicole said, shocked.

"Did you get drunk and have to be driven home?"

"Well, I probably wasn't in the best shape to drive, so Salil drove me home," Nicole said. "It's not like I was swinging from the lights and doing catcalls, though," she added, trying to lighten the tone.

"I'm not sure if what I heard was much better." Paul sighed, looking down at his desk.

"What are you talking about?" Nicole demanded, sitting up straighter in her chair.

"Why were you dancing on the table, singing into the light, and exposing yourself to your coworkers?"

"Excuse me?"

"Surely you know that's probably not the best behavior for a manager, and I know this is somewhat personal, but really? No bra either?"

"What the hell? You heard I was dancing on the table without a bra?"

"Yes, what prompted you?"

Aghast, Nicole just sat there with her mouth open. After blinking a couple of times, she finally spoke. "First, I did *not* get up on a table, and second, I did *not* take my bra off or attend a company function without one on! After two kids, these mamasitas need support!"

"Are you sure you remember everything? I heard you were pretty drunk," Paul said, trying to sympathize.

"Yes, I'm sure!"

"Well, then tell me about your unhealthy obsession with our CIO," Paul prompted.

"What do you mean 'unhealthy obsession'?" Nicole spat out.

"Look, it's just not okay to say you want to show our CIO your red Santa thong and give him a lap dance. It gives the wrong impression, and when people on your team hear that, you're going to lose respect."

"What are you talking about? I never said *anything* about a lap dance or a red Santa thong. What is going on here? Am I on candid camera, Paul?" Nicole flipped her head, looking around the office for the camera, trying to make her point.

"How often do misunderstandings like this happen?"

"What do you mean?" she stammered, still looking around with eyes wide scanning the room.

"I mean, how often after one of your nights out do you find people telling stories that aren't true about you?"

[PAUL'S NOTE: *Do you see where I was trying to go? I was thinking that if these kinds of stories always followed her after a night of drinking, maybe she was too drunk to really remember everything clearly and that she needed an intervention.*]

[NICOLE'S NOTE: *That's why you asked me that?*]

[PAUL'S NOTE: *Hey, I still wasn't sure you weren't just trying to pull the wool over my eyes. I was truly coming from a good place and trying to help.*]

[NICOLE'S NOTE: *Whatever, Saint Paul.*]

"Never. I've never been accused of dancing on a table, showing my boobs, and wanting to make a pass at my CIO before. I can't believe you're even asking me all this. Who told you that's what happened?"

"It doesn't matter. Just some concerned teammates."

"Oh, it matters, because someone's lying," Nicole fired back, red hot like the candy now. She had to clear her besmirched name to Paul and then quickly begin damage control on this rumor before it got out of control. Nicole called Ava.

"Hey, girl, what's up?" Ava said in her sassy, Boston accent.

"Guuuurrrlll, you would not believe the mess I have come into this morning!" Nicole fumed, not letting her in on the fact that Paul was right there and listening in.

"Oh my God, what's going on?" Ava responded, now clearly hearing the seriousness in Nicole's voice.

"I came into the office and Paul is telling me that I'm a lush who was hanging out last night, dancing on tables, singing into chandeliers, showing my Nicolettes, and bragging about how I'm going to give our CIO a lap dance. Can you believe it?" Nicole's voice was full of animation and disbelief.

"*What?* Who said that?" Ava replied, shocked by the accusations.

"Yes, girl, that's what my team told Paul this morning!"

"No, they didn't! You were nothing like that. Here's what happened." And Ava began to relay the story. Nicole simply arched her eyebrow at Paul, pushed the speakerphone button and pointed at the speaker for him to pay attention.

"At some point, a song came on and you were like, 'That is my jam', and then you started singing into the little sconce on the wall next to your chair. By no means were you up on a table."

As Ava retold the rest of the story, Nicole continued to give Paul "you gullible dumbass" and the "how the hell could you believe this crap about me?" looks. Ava went on about how someone said something to Nicole about her top and how she showed them the heavy, brown tank top that was under it (which was a far cry from the rumor of her top being see-through or not having a bra on). There was also zero mention about a Santa Claus thong or a lap dance.

By the time Ava was done, Nicole was exonerated and Paul was the one who was red hot. Before the call ended, Ava asked, "Do you know who started these rumors?"

Paul spoke up. "Well, Brenda was the spokesperson for the team this morning."

"Paul, I didn't know you were there. Brenda, huh? Well, that explains that," Ava responded flatly. "It figures. Nicole, I am really sorry, girl. I saw Brenda this morning, and she asked how things went last night. I told her about some of the things that went on, and she must have added her own embellishments to the story. Mmnt. I hate that your team is trying to get you into rehab!"

"That phisher! Oh, I could beat the seven shades of shit out of her right now! Girl, they are trying to do more than rehab. They are trying to get me on a twelve-step program!" Nicole responded, trying to make light of the situation.

"Wait. Phisher…what's that?" Ava asked.

"A phisher is the office gossip. You know, the person who fishes around for gossip and then exaggerates what they caught," Nicole explained.

Paul and Ava both let out hearty laughs, now understanding that the situation wasn't at all what it was made out to be.

Once they hung up with Ava, it was time for Nicole to confront her team.

Nicole explained how she called Ava without telling her Paul was in the room and how Ava corroborated her story of the night before. She added that had she really been that sloppy drunk, she wouldn't have been able to make it into work.

Most important, she thanked her team for being concerned enough about her to bring the situation to her manager and friend. Nicole let them know that by no means was she upset or disappointed in them. If she had heard these same stories, she would have been concerned, too. She then reminded them that the thing about office rumors is just that: they are rumors, often retold with embellishments to make the story more appetizing.

"The story always sounds better when you've caught a shark versus a sardine," Nicole added.

Sighs of relief ensued and, before long, they were all hugging and praising eight-pound, six-ounce Baby Jesus that Nicole wasn't a lush. Then all of a sudden, someone said, "Well, I guess we should give her our gift after all."

"Gift? Who has a gift? You guys got me a gift?" Nicole blushed.

"Of course we did," they sung in unison. "You've been the best manager a group could ask for, and we are just totally thankful to have you. You're so much fun, you look out for us, you stand by us, and you're just fantastic. We love you! There's no one better!" Each of them took turns offering up their praise and adoration.

[PAUL'S NOTE: *"Just fantastic...there's no one better." Really?*]
[NICOLE'S NOTE: *This is my memory, and that's how I remember it.*]
[PAUL'S NOTE: *Somehow I don't think it was quite like that.*]
[NICOLE'S NOTE: *Were you there?*]
[PAUL'S NOTE: *Well, no, but—*]
[NICOLE'S NOTE: *Then just take it as is...white bread! That's why you weren't invited to the after party.*]
[PAUL'S NOTE: *You know, that's cold. Out in the rain in the middle of December cold. It hurts...deep.*]

[NICOLE'S NOTE: *Whatever. <eyes rolling>*]

Antoinette pulled out a green box with a bow.

"Is that what I think it is? Is it...*yes, it is!*" Nicole exclaimed. "You love me. You really love me, don't you?" Nicole carefully unwrapped a beautiful new bottle of Patrón, her favorite tequila, and promised them that they wouldn't see her on the eleven o'clock news.

As the days went on, though, the story of Nicole and her Santa's thong continued to surface, each one a little different than the last. In some stories, she had on a sheer camisole with a leopard-print bra. In other versions, her top was sheer with no bra. All of them, though, had some variation of her singing into a chandelier, sconce, or candle, and all of them had something about Santa, the CIO, and a lap dance.

Nicole was mortified when she finally saw her CIO at the managers' holiday party a couple of weeks later. Unsure of what to say, she just looked at him. He came right up to her, put his arm around her shoulder, and simply said, "Yes, I've heard the rumors, and no, I don't believe them. We all know where they originated, and we all know to ignore her stories. However, I do want to know what a Santa Claus thong is!" And with that, he let out a huge laugh, gave her shoulder a final squeeze, and called out the next manager's name as he continued to work the room and talk to his peeps.

Swim at your Own Risk

The problem about gossiping is that it's always at someone else's expense, pure and simple. While embellishing a story may make it more tantalizing, embellishments could have negative ramifications. Take Nicole's situation. Had her CIO believed the stories he heard, she could have easily been terminated.

Be careful to not become the office phisher. Although everyone loves to hear gossip, being known as the gossiper isn't an accomplishment to be proud of. Think of it this way: though fishing can be a lucrative business, fishing in the wrong holes could cause you to drown!

Here are a few key tenets to keep in mind when the opportunity to fish comes to your watering hole:

Was the phish received firsthand?

There's a big difference between hearing something firsthand and having it told to you. When receiving the dish, think about who's cooking it. Is it someone who regularly embellishes a story (i.e. the person who's eager to retell the story because he or she likes being in the middle of the mess)? This isn't the same as attention whores, who simply love for people to like them (like Nicole); no, this person is likely to *not* be the center of attention unless he or she is telling juicy gossip and always stirring the pot.

So you caught the phish?

If you were there, and saw it with your own eyes, and heard it with your own ears--and it's funny--and it won't cause any potential harm, then by all means, phish away!

[NICOLE'S NOTE: *Remember gay neck?*]

However, if the story could be damaging, be mindful as to whether this is a story that needs repeating, especially if it's at a company event or with coworkers. Remember, the Santa Claus thong story could have left Nicole and her wee ones standing out in the cold, jobless, husband-less, and without Christmas cheer!

Trimming the Fat

Keep the gossipers at bay by always being honest and upfront in your interactions with people. Don't embellish stories to try to get ahead because it always backfires. (Remember the rule of karma: she's a bitch, and she's taking names and keeping score.)

Bringing Up the Rear

Before we share our potluck secrets and before you go and throw your hooves high into the air and inject yourself (and others) into the fabulous lane of life, we want to ensure you've prepared your kitchen (your attitude), turned on your oven (adjusted your outlook), and are ready to bake up and eat something wonderful (allow the good things that follow to flow).

People have said for years that laughter is the best medicine, yet so many people take life (especially work life) too seriously to see the humor in it all. It's there, waiting to relieve day-to-day pressures and stresses; you just have to open up to see it. Whether it's your shirt on backward or panties that ride up, those little blips in the day can take the edge off and add longevity to life.

[NICOLE'S NOTE: Really, Paul?!]
[PAUL'S NOTE: What?]
[NICOLE'S NOTE: All the examples used are of me and my mishaps! What about yours!?]
[PAUL'S NOTE: Well, I can't help it that I pay more attention to my wardrobe when leaving the house. Besides, these are great lessons our fellow Hoofers can learn from your mishaps. Think of it as helping! <Insert model smile>]
[NICOLE'S NOTE: Mmmnt!]

You now have the tools needed to be an honorary Hoofer. As you go back to the cube farm, think of how you can create a balance between workday stress and impromptu fun through laughter. Ask yourself if you're laughing enough and whether or not you are creating or contributing to a fun, happy atmosphere for your friends, coworkers and employees.

We've spent much of this book celebrating food, so we'd be remiss if we didn't guide you through a perfect potluck. But first, you must take the Hoofer Pledge:

> *I, <state your name>, do promise and swear on the country ham that I will find at least one thing in the cube farm to add a smile to my face and a tickle to my heart. I promise to engage others, both in and out of my team, to participate in themed potlucks and encourage them to open up and let loose. I pledge to be friendly, fun, and increase the morale of those around me and myself as well. Finally, I promise to convert my friends and family to become fellow Hoofers so long as the pig shall live!*

Perfect Potlucks

Introduction

We've spent much of this book celebrating food—oh, how we love it—and shared with you our funny stories that have revolved around it. Potlucks are not only a great way to feed your love for food (and feed ourselves—LOL), but it's also a great way to feed your relationships with others: members of your team, members of other teams you want to develop a better working relationship with, or friends and family members outside of the office.

We always start small by involving our teams first. After the first couple of potlucks, word will get around that you and your team are doing something fun and enjoying lots of great food.

[NICOLE'S NOTE: *We also like to leave the door of the conference room open and make loud statements about how great the food is and how much fun we're having.*]

[PAUL'S NOTE: *We can hear you saying, "Mmnt!" Stop it. It's part of the plan.*]

Sure, there will be snide comments from the ones who add a splash of Hater-Ade in their coffee and tea every day, but you'll quickly find other people and teams who want to join in. Invite them! The more, the merrier!

[NICOLE'S NOTE: *And the more food and potluck opportunities you'll have!*]

Once you have a few teams, you can increase the number of potlucks you have by having people bring in a dish only every other potluck or every third potluck. (And who doesn't love coming to a potluck where you don't have to bring anything?)

[PAUL'S NOTE: *Me! Hooves High! EYB!*]
[NICOLE'S NOTE: *Me too! Eight pounds, six ounces!*]

You'll find that after hosting several of these, you'll have a large number of people joining in. More important, you'll have a large number of people you can now reach out to when you have a task you need help with or a project with a tight deadline. We're certainly not encouraging going around a process, but we are saying you catch more flies with honey.

[PAUL'S NOTE: *Lord, yes, don't ever go around a process. Nicole and I build and implement processes for a living, so don't be putting us out on the street by not following them!*]

Perfect Potluck Prerequisites
If you're hosting a potluck at work, there are some prerequisites, or rules, you need to abide by:

1. Respect your company's lunch policy. If lunch is one hour, like most are, ensure you stick to that so you don't piss off the powers-that-be. It's fine if people need to drop by a little earlier to set up, but keep the eating and the cleaning up within the appropriate time limits.

2. Plan potlucks over a common lunch hour, like 11:30–12:30, 12:00–1:00, or 12:30–1:30.
3. If you or your team are hosting the potluck, it's your responsibility to direct everyone to the plates, utensils, and grub. If you've invited others who may not be familiar with some people at the potluck, escort them to a table and make some introductions. They'll appreciate it and may be in a position to return the favor one day.

[NICOLE'S NOTE: *Yes, you never know who has a hookup with one of the Cs—you know, the CEO, CIO, CFO, or CTO.*]

Perfect Potluck Occasions

Obviously, if potlucks are something new for you or your team, or even, God forbid, your company, you'll need to start by commemorating large holidays such as these ten favorites:

- **New Year's Day (January 1)**
  This is the time of year when all Hoofers get self-conscious about embracing their bigness and decide to embrace rice cakes and lettuce instead. A good Hoofer is nothing if not supportive (even during misguided attempts such as these), so plan a "skinny potluck" where people bring in their favorite low-calorie or low-fat foods to show your encouragement.
- **Martin Luther King Jr.'s Birthday (third Monday in January)**
  By the third week in January, we know you'll be done embracing your skinniness, so use MLK's birthday as a "Welcome Back to the Herd" party. To pay tribute to this great southern leader, invite all to bring their best southern dishes. We're talking about fried chicken, Mama's Mac 'n Cheese, collard

greens, corn bread, and sweet tea. Maybe even throw in a couple of fried Oreos and fried Twinkies for good measure. Everything is better fried. *Everything!*

- **Valentine's Day (February 14)**
  Valentine's Day is all about doing something sweet for that special someone, so why not have a potluck dedicated to sweets? Nothing says love like a few extra pounds, because the more of you there is, the more there is to love, so eat an extra piece of cake or pie for us.

  [PAUL'S NOTE: *Being an all-dessert potluck, it's my favorite for obvious reasons.*]

- **Easter (first Sunday following the Paschal Full Moon)**
  To rejoice the fact that Lent is over and you can now have all those foods you'd banned yourself from for the last forty days, arrange a "forbidden potluck," where everyone brings in the food they'd sworn off. If they didn't swear off a food or didn't participate in Lent, it doesn't matter. Just have them bring in their most tantalizing temptation! Everyone's hooves will be high, and those so inclined will also be honoring the resurrection of the Lord as they squeal, "Eight-pound, six-ounce Baby Jesus!" in delight.

- **Memorial Day (last Monday in May)**
  Memorial Day marks the beginning of summer and the first chance to whip out the grill and bring in some hot dogs, hamburgers, and homemade barbecue. Even though we fully support our little pig mascot, we have no trouble throwing some pork on the barbie and smothering it with vinegar- or mustard-based barbeque sauce. Just don't forget to invite us when you do, okay?

- **Fourth of July (July 4—duh)**
  All things red, white, and blue are approved for this potluck. Commemorate America's independence with some red velvet

cake, blueberry muffins, strawberry shortcake, deviled eggs, or cherry Jell-O shooters (if it's after work, of course). We hold this truth to be self-evident: "If there's no fat, no sugar, no dairy...it's no good; throw it out!"

- **Labor Day (first Monday in September)**
  Honor the Labor Day holiday with an easy-peasy potluck to keep you from having to work too hard. Only bring in foods that take less than fifteen minutes to prepare, like our Shiznit Spinach Dip or our Canna Cake (both of which we include in the next chapter).
- **Halloween (October 31)**
  If your workplace will allow it, host a costume contest and have participants parade around during the potluck, trying to scare up votes. If you're feeling adventurous and have a lot of eager ghouls, include a cube-decorating contest and send an e-mail tempting others to come by and help judge. Stir up some Slimy Limey Fruit Punch or Bone Chilling Brew to lure people into your web of ghoulish delight.

[NICOLE'S NOTE: *One year when Paul forced our teams into a pirate theme, I was the sexy Tia Dalma from* Pirates of the Caribbean: Dead Man's Chest. *The good news is I won the contest. Not that I'm surprised. I was fabulous!*]

[PAUL'S NOTE: *Good grief! Now you're sexy and fabulous? We're near the end of this book, and where are my adjectives? Can I get a "Yes, you are a long, tall drink of a man" or "handsome" "boyish" or "gorgeous" please? Mmnt!*]

[NICOLE'S NOTE: *From me? Uh, no. I might be persuaded to say "reliable", "dependable", "skilled" and "positive", though.*]

[PAUL'S NOTE: *Really? None of those allude at all to my sexiness or hotness like your adjectives do!*]

[NICOLE'S NOTE: *No shit, Sherlock.*]

[PAUL'S NOTE: *Keep digging, Watson, because I am all those things!*]
[NICOLE'S NOTE: *Very nice.*]

- **Thanksgiving (fourth Thursday in November)**
  Bring on the turkey, bring on the ham, bring on the stuffing, and bring on the biscuits and jam! Just don't exceed the feed limit as you're gorging on all the wonderful treats from your potluck bounty. With so much good food, you already know you're going to be in a food coma, and it won't be cute if you have to be rolled back to your desk afterward.
- **Christmas/Hanukkah/Kwanzaa (December)**
  The options are endless for a Christmas, Hanukkah, and Kwanzaa potluck. Most employers are feeling generous at this time of year, so totally take advantage of that and schedule something off site or, at the very least, for a couple of hours so you have time to socialize and play some games. This is also the perfect opportunity to hit your leadership team up to pay for the big-ticket items, like the meat. If they won't or act reluctant, we're not above telling you to guilt them into it. They make you work like a dog all year long, and the least they can do now is throw you a bone in the shape of a nice roasted turkey or honey-baked ham.

  [PAUL'S NOTE: *And don't forget my fabulous Merry Christmas Cookies! They'll be the talk and toast of your holiday festivities!*]
  [NICOLE'S NOTE: *Yeah, they'll be talking about how they need more punch to get rid of that salty taste!*]

Once you've gotten everyone accustomed to the standard potluck days, start digging deeper. There is a plethora of other holidays you can celebrate. We suggest the following additional ten holidays, but really, you just need a willingness to plan it and have enough peeps to participate:

- **Groundhog Day (February 2)**
  Let's be honest. No one wants that fat little rodent to see his shadow in February and force six more weeks of winter on us. We say celebrate with a Groundhog Day "souptacular" where everyone brings in soup or some other cold-weather favorite to ward off any more cold mornings where our cars won't start and our fingers are too frozen to de-ice the driveways.
- **Washington's Birthday (February 22)**
  If you scoff at this, then you are scoffing at the very fabric of our great nation and its Founding Fathers. George Washington's birthday is a great time to have your organization's best bakers bring in their most charming cherry pies, cherry tarts, cherry fritters, and cherry cobblers. Let everyone judge the wares, vote on their favorite, and award a first prize in each category as well as a best in show. Little Georgie knew what he was doing when he chopped down that cherry tree to get to its yummy fruit!
- **April Fool's Day (April 1)**
  This is one of our favorite potlucks! Have people bring in their craziest, wildest, and most unusual concoctions that look weird, but are really quite tasty. It's fun food to fool people with! The ones that top our list are Bird Poop (made from peanut butter crunch cereal, rice crisp cereal, pretzels, white chocolate, and mini marshmallows), Cat Barf (made from spaghetti squash, cottage cheese, mozzarella, parmesan, spaghetti sauce, and green peppers), and Dog Food Dip (made from ground beef, onions, cream of mushroom soup, cheese, and jalapenos).

[NICOLE'S NOTE: *Or you could just bring in your salty cookies. The joke will be on them for sure then!*]

[PAUL'S NOTE: *Mmnt! Bitch 'bout to get some* salt *thrown in her eyes!*]

- **Earth Day (April 22)**
  Who wouldn't want to come to a party to honor the planet? To pay tribute, have everyone bring their dishes in containers made with recycled containers and only use plates, napkins, and utensils made from earth-friendly materials. As Kermit the Frog says, it's good to be green.
- **Administrative Assistant's Day (Wednesday in the last full week in April)**
  We all know these are the hardest-working and most under-appreciated people in any organization. They run around keeping everyone and everything organized and running smoothly, so why not invite them to a potluck in their honor? It's the perfect present because you get to enjoy it just as much as they do.
- **Mother's Day (second Sunday in May)**
  Let the ladies off the hook, and make the guys bring in all the food for this one. You may end up with a lot of grilled items or things they begged their wives to bake for them, but it's the thought that counts, right?
- **Father's Day (third Sunday in June)**
  It's the ladies' turn to cook for the men. It's bound to be better than what the men brought, but you know they'll still act like theirs was better.

[NICOLE'S NOTE: *Yes, just like in an argument. Men always think they're right, but we ladies know that if they ever win, it's because we let them…or we just got too tired of listening to their sorry asses try.*]

- **Columbus Day (October 12)**
  Christopher Columbus may not have had much to eat when he was crossing the Atlantic back in 1492, but that doesn't mean you can't celebrate with a feast of Italian favorites, like lasagna and spaghetti, to celebrate his heritage. *Delizioso!*
- **United Nations Day (October 24)**
  Here's a great opportunity to have all your multicultural or ethnic coworkers cook their favorite dishes and bring them in for you to try. Have you ever had authentic Chinese Chop Suey or Indian Pudding? Yum!
- **Veterans Day (November 11)**
  In war, there is no prize for runner-up, so only have people bring in their blue-ribbon best dishes for this extravaganza. Honor the men and women who've fought bravely for our country and thank them as they come in. Let them go through the food line first and give them a place of distinction to eat among the civilians.

Perfect Potluck Matrix

There's nothing easier than a potluck. It allows groups of people to come together in fellowship and, best of all, when it's done, cleanup is a cinch because everyone just takes their dishes back home!

[PAUL'S NOTE: *Praise little eight-pound, six-ounce Baby Jesus for easy cleanups!*]

However, your potluck can quickly go from fabulous to fucked if a little bit of coordination isn't done up front. The last thing you want is a potluck where everyone's expecting a little bit of everything, and instead all you've got is a whole lot of one thing, like dessert.

[NICOLE'S NOTE: *While I fully support dessert, I also expect to have some gravy and a little somethin'—that is, somethin' to pour it over! There's nothing better than a potato pool where there's so much heffa juice, you can barely see the whites of the potatoes!*]

To prevent your potluck from dessert overload, we have developed the foolproof Perfect Potluck Matrix.

[PAUL'S NOTE: *Mmnt! This is a bad example. I'd be just fine with a dessert overload, but whatever. Carry on.*]

A successful potluck is the result of careful organization, planning, and direction. Someone must be in charge to ensure all palates are taken care of and that everyone participates. A potluck organizer is never successful without a supporting cast of minions, so we recommend creating an Events Committee that will be responsible for organizing all events, from baby showers to potlucks. This is a great idea because it brings people together in a work setting to bond over something that's not necessarily work-related. Rotate people off the committee periodically to allow others a chance to participate. We can't emphasize the importance of having someone in charge of the establishment of a committee, though, because there's nothing worse than finding out you've got a ton of great food and no plates or utensils to eat it with!

[NICOLE'S NOTE: *That's right! 'Cause Lord knows you can't eat gravy with your fingers! And it's too hot to pour into your hand!*]
[PAUL'S NOTE: *Speaking from experience, are we?*]
[NICOLE'S NOTE: *I burned the fingerprint off my right index finger. Let's just move on.*]

The first thing you must do is get a head count. Knowing how big your herd is will be crucial for the success of the potluck matrix, but also for booking the proper size venue (i.e. conference room). Just like a home-thrown function, there's nothing more embarrassing than not having enough food or enough seats. Hoofers do not appreciate having to stand around and burn calories while they eat. No, they enjoy sitting and absorbing all of their calories instead.

There are three categories to the matrix: Name, Food Type, and the actual Dish Name. The Name column is where the individual's name is placed when they sign up for an item.

There are typically six Food Types: appetizers/fruit/salad, meat, starch, veggie, dessert, and plates/utensils. Depending on how large your group is, you might break appetizer/fruit/salad into two or three additional Food Types. By providing a list of the Food Types upfront, you're setting peoples' expectations on what to bring (the boundaries) and allowing them to sign up for the Food Type that makes them happiest.

Now, you'll notice there's not an item for drinks. This is because, as true Hoofers, drinks are wasted calories and therefore a wasted category. Paul and Nicole would much rather have another dessert or amazing appetizer than a soda. That's what vending machines and water fountains are for. However, if your company does not provide vending machines or water fountains (yes, crappy companies like that exist), feel free to update the matrix accordingly.

The final column is the Dish Name column. The purpose of this column is twofold. First, it ensures that if two people sign up to bring a starch item, they don't both bring the same starch. Who wants two pans of mashed potatoes when you could have both mashed potatoes *and* macaroni and cheese? Second, and more important, it allows fellow Hoofers the opportunity to plan their course of action on which foods they're going to eat and in which order.

Below is an example of a completed matrix:

Name	Food Type	Dish Name
Chandra	Appetizer/Fruit/Salad	Seafood Pasta Salad
Marilyn	Appetizer/Fruit/Salad	Assorted Melon Plate
Kenneth	Meat	BBQ Pulled Pork
Ryan	Meat	Meatballs
Rian	Meat	Chicken
Theo	Starch	German Potato Salad
Megan	Starch	Sausage/Rice dish
Autumn	Veggie	Baked Beans
Gabi	Veggie	Corn
Marie	Veggie	Grilled Veggies
Paul	Dessert	Chocolate Surprise
Susan	Dessert	Marzipan Cake
Nancy	Dessert	Peach Cobbler
Ali	Plates/Utensils	Plates/Utensils

Okay, so now that you've got a matrix, you're probably wondering how to determine how many of each Food Type to have. This is where knowing the number of people involved comes into play. For every group of ten people, you should have the following:

- One (1) Appetizer/Fruit/Salad
- Two (2) Meats
- Two (2) Starches

- Two (2) Veggies
- Two (2) Desserts

A great start to any meal is an appetizer. However, there should never be too many of them, especially if your potluck is during a lunch hour. It's hard for a Hoofer to get full off nuts and berries, and there's nothing worse than a hungry herd!

Of course, numbers should be adjusted accordingly. For instance, if your numbers are between ten and twenty, you'll want to increase the number of meats and vegetables first. Starches, while good, also have a great deal of sugar in them. If you're increasing your dessert numbers, you don't want to increase the starches first, but instead the appetizers to offset the sugar intake. Conversely, if your crowd is a bunch of hungry men who don't care as much for desserts, then increase your starches and appetizers first and then the desserts. Regardless of the number of participants, meats and vegetables should always be increased before the other Food Type items.

Once you've got your matrix figured out, you're ready to send a note to the masses with all the potluck details. Make sure the instructions are clear, though, or all your efforts will be in vain. Instruct people to only respond back to the person managing the matrix.

[PAUL'S NOTE: *Yes, no one wants to see a hundred e-mails flying back and forth about who's bringing what. Spam is bad—both the e-mail practice and the food. I think it goes without saying that you should never bring Spam to a potluck.*]

Next—and pay attention to this one, people—ensure everyone knows the signup is on a first-come, first-take basis. If your lazy ass waits until the last minute to sign up for plates and utensils and all that's left is meat, oh well, it sucks to be you! Hit the local grocery store and pick up the ingredients for Miracle Meatballs. If you really wanted appetizers and all that's left is dessert, shoulda, coulda, woulda, but cha didn't, so hit a bakery and keep it movin'! There are no excuses here!

[NICOLE'S NOTE: *Yes, as Ricky Bobby says, "If you're not first, you're last!"*]

[PAUL'S NOTE: *Really? We're quoting fictional characters in our book now?*]

[NICOLE'S NOTE: *I don't know what the problem is. If Olivia or Beyoncé said it, we wouldn't be having this conversation. MMNT!*]

[PAUL'S NOTE: *WTH? They are both real people. Ricky Bobby isn't even real.*]

[NICOLE'S NOTE: *I let you have your fantasies. And trust me, while Olivia and B might be real, neither of them will ever snatch you away to become their love-slave boy toy like you hope. Just like Ricky will never snatch me away to be his backup driver. What now, Wonder Bread?*]

[PAUL'S NOTE: *<silence>*]

[NICOLE'S NOTE: *That's what I thought. Mmnt.*]

Periodically send an e-mail with the updated matrix. This allows those who have yet to sign up to see what's already been taken and may possibly motivate them to sign up for something before all the good slots are gone. It also satisfies the Hoofers who want to know what they'll be eating. A week out, send a reminder specifically to those individuals who have yet to sign up, letting them know what's available. There will always be a few slackers who wait until the last minute. Keep in mind, you don't want to embarrass them or call them out; no one wants saliva seasoning in the heffa juice!

Finally, send a simple reminder to the entire group with the completed matrix a couple of days before the potluck event. Its purpose is to remind people the potluck is a couple of days away and that if they haven't already picked up the ingredients or their item, they've only got a couple of days left to do so.

That's it! Any Hoofer can do it or delegate it to someone else!

[NICOLE'S NOTE: *Folks, it really is that simple.*]

[PAUL'S NOTE: *It really is.*]

[NICOLE'S NOTE: *Excuse me! How would you know?*]

[PAUL'S NOTE: *What? I've seen you do it. It didn't look that hard to me. A trained monkey could do it.*]

[NICOLE'S NOTE: *Are you calling me a monkey, now?*]

[PAUL'S NOTE: *That's not what I said. However, you do constantly pull stuff off of people, like hair and lint.*]

[NICOLE'S NOTE: *<sucks teeth with raised eyebrow—the cut-a-bitch look> I'll deal with you later!*]

[PAUL'S NOTE: *Bring it!*]

[NICOLE'S NOTE: *Oh, it's been brought!*]

[PAUL'S NOTE: *Very nice.*]

Perfect Potluck Recipes

Introduction

First of all, let us just say you are privileged and special to be able to cast your eyes upon these recipes. Their secret ingredients have been handed down from generation to generation, and Paul's Great-Grandma Sarah and Nicole's Great-Oma Anna would be rolling over in their graves if they knew we were committing these to paper.

Oh, hell, who are we kidding? These aren't tried-and-true beloved family recipes. We don't even know where they all came from. We just inherited them from other great Hoofers who like to eat, too, but we'll sure as shit try to take credit for them now!

Below, you'll find recipes for two each of our absolute favorite appetizers, entrées, side dishes, and desserts. In addition, we've included the three April Fool's and two Halloween recipes we mentioned earlier. They're super easy to make, and if these can't make you look good, you're a mental midget. Sorry, but it's true.

[PAUL'S NOTE: *But wait, there's more! I'm also including the recipe for my famous Merry Christmas Cookies so you can judge for yourself whether they're really salty!*]

[NICOLE'S NOTE: *Really? We're going to have to reduce the price of this book now. Hello, bargain bin.*]

[PAUL'S NOTE: *Mmnt! I am done with you! D-O-N-E! Done! Just make them yourself and try them before passing judgment. That's all I'm saying.*]

Shiznit Spinach Dip

First brought to one of Nicole's house parties (thanks, Libby), this dip has turned into a potluck favorite! Served cold, not hot, this dip is far from a cold fish! Couple it with some scoopable corn chips, and You'll notice people flocking to the bowl and "mmm hmmms" flying around!

GET IT OUT

- 1 package chopped frozen spinach
- 8 oz. sour cream
- 1 cup mayo
- 1 packet Hidden Valley Ranch mix
- Artichokes or bacon (if desired)

WHIP IT UP

- Thaw the spinach, draining all water.
- Mix all ingredients in a large bowl.
- Chill and serve.
- Add additional items, like artichokes or bacon, as desired.

◆ ◆ ◆

Buffalo Chicken Dip

This is the best kind of appetizer. It's hot, messy, and can cause trouble if you eat too much of it. Marilyn's sister, Dee, introduced Paul to it, and he absconded with the recipe and claimed it as his own at the very next potluck. It was an instant hit, and with only five ingredients and one bowl, it's quick and easy, like a drunken bridesmaid at a wedding.

GET IT OUT

- 2 (15 oz.) cans chicken (or you can use cooked, diced chicken breasts)
- 2 (8 oz.) packages cream cheese
- ¾ cup ranch dressing (not the dry packets)
- ½ cup (or more) buffalo wing sauce
- ½ cup shredded cheddar cheese

WHIP IT UP

- Mix all ingredients together and spread in a 9 × 13 pan.
- Bake at 350 degrees until bubbly.
- Add more shredded cheese on top when it's done.
- Serve with tortillas or corn chips.

Miracle Meatballs

Nicole calls these Miracle Meatballs because after she makes them, it's a miracle she can move out of the way fast enough before the congregation tramples her down. She's never made a batch of these and had even a single meatball left. Hallelujah!

GET IT OUT

- 1 package frozen meatballs (around 60)
- 1 bottle Sweet Baby Ray's honey barbecue sauce

- Cane syrup to taste (maple syrup will also do)
- ½ cup brown sugar

WHIP IT UP

- Place all ingredients in a standard Crock-Pot and let simmer for 6 hours. The end result should have a sweet flavor, so add more brown sugar or syrup to taste.

[NICOLE'S NOTE: *Oh, and Mama loves her some big, juicy balls. Mmm, Mmmm, Mmmm! Meatballs, people, meatballs. Get your minds out of the gutter!*]

◆ ◆ ◆

Baked Ziti

Oh cheese, glorious cheese! We're talking about the kind of cheese that is so gooey and wonderful that it can fill the cracks of a broken heart and make it brand new again. Have a significant other who dumped you? Baked ziti. Have a pet that passed? Baked ziti. Done the cry of a lonesome turd (i.e., farted) at the most inappropriate time during a meeting with your new boss you've only known for five seconds? Baked ziti. And it was loud and caused him to wrinkle his nose due to the smell? Add more cheese.

GET IT OUT

- 3 cups dry ziti pasta
- ½ lb. ground beef or turkey
- 3 cups spaghetti sauce
- 2 cups cottage cheese
- 2 tbsp. grated parmesan cheese

- 1 egg
- 1 tsp. dried parsley
- ¼ tsp. garlic powder
- 4 cups mozzarella cheese (Hooves High!)

WHIP IT UP

- Cook the ziti according to the package directions, omitting the salt and oil.
- Crumble meat in a large skillet sprayed with a nonstick cooking spray.
- Sauté until the meat is cooked, stirring frequently.
- Add spaghetti sauce to the meat.
- In a separate bowl, combine cottage cheese, Parmesan cheese, egg, parsley, and garlic powder. Mix thoroughly.
- Add the ziti to the cheese mixture and mix well.
- Spread 1 cup of the meat sauce in the bottom of a 9 × 13 baking pan that has been sprayed with nonstick cooking spray.
- Sprinkle 2 cups of mozzarella cheese over the meat sauce.
- Spoon the ziti and cheese mixture over the mozzarella cheese.
- Spread remaining meat sauce over the ziti and cheese mixture.
- Sprinkle remaining 2 cups of mozzarella cheese over the top.

BAKE IT, BITCH!

- Cover with aluminum foil and bake for 30 minutes at 350 degrees.

Mama's Mac 'N Cheese

Paul's mama, Nancy, can cook like nobody's business (she can also clean a house like nobody's business, in heels, but that's another story). When Paul was younger, she cooked three squares a day. Nothing came pre-done from a box (and still doesn't today). She peeled and mashed her own potatoes by hand, made and rolled her own dough for biscuits, and picked her own blackberries for blackberry cobbler. She loves new recipes and isn't afraid to try anything, but once she's found the best, she's got it, and it becomes a staple in her menus. When we tell you this mac 'n cheese recipe beat out dozens of others, trust us, it did. We're even giving you the version where you don't have to make your own noodles (lucky for you she does approve of store-bought noodles—LOL).

GET IT OUT

- 2 cups cottage cheese
- 8 oz. sour cream
- 1 large egg, beaten
- ¾ tsp. salt
- ½ tsp. pepper
- 4 cups shredded cheese
- 8 oz. package elbow macaroni, cooked and drained

WHIP IT UP

- Mix the cottage cheese, sour cream, egg, salt, pepper, and 2 cups of shredded cheese together in a large bowl.
- Stir in the cooked macaroni.
- Spread the mixture into a greased, 2-quart baking dish.

BAKE IT, BITCH!

- Bake at 325 degrees for 40 minutes. During the last 10 minutes of baking, add the remaining 2 cups of shredded cheese to the top.

Whoosh! Whoosh! That's the sound of your arteries clogging and dying a happy death!

◆ ◆ ◆

Karen's Kick-Ass Sweet Potato Soufflé

We actually do know where this one came from, but we're not sure if Karen's mother made it up or if she bummed it off someone herself. Regardless, Karen's getting credit because she introduced it to us. It's her kick-ass sweet potato soufflé, and let us tell you, it is the fluffiest mound of goodness we have ever tasted. In fact, we're going to have to take a break from writing this just so we can go make some now. Eight pounds, six ounces!

[NICOLE'S NOTE: *And we did.*]
[PAUL'S NOTE: *And Nicole left hoof prints in the dish. He-he.*]

GET IT OUT

Soufflé Mix

- 4 cups mashed and cooked sweet potatoes
- 1 cup sugar
- ½ cup melted butter

- 2 beaten eggs
- 1 tbsp. vanilla
- $^1/_3$ cup evaporated milk

Topping

- 1 cup brown sugar
- ½ cup flour
- $^1/_3$ cup melted butter
- 1 cup chopped nuts

WHIP IT UP

- Mix the soufflé ingredients together in a large bowl. Spread evenly into casserole dish.
- Mix all the topping ingredients together in medium bowl and sprinkle the topping over soufflé.

BAKE IT, BITCH!

- Bake at 350 degrees for 25 minutes.

Chocolate Surprise

As we mentioned earlier in this book, this is Paul's favorite dessert—*ever!* It's not hard to make, but it does take a little planning. There are many versions of this recipe out there, several with fruit, but Paul's a chocolate man, so this version is made with full-fat chocolate pudding. I'm sure you could use the fat-free kind, but why? Once you see the rest of the ingredients, you'll understand. EYB!

GET IT OUT

Crust

- 1½ cups flour
- 1½ sticks butter, melted
- 1 cup chopped pecans

Creamy Layer

- 12 oz. cream cheese
- 1½ cups powdered sugar
- 9 oz. whipped topping

Chocolaty Goodness Layer

- 2 small boxes instant chocolate pudding

Whipped Topping Layer

- 1 pint whipping cream
- ½ cup powdered sugar

[PAUL'S NOTE: *Now I know what you're thinking. We're already using whipped topping in the creamy layer. Can't I just buy more and use it on top? No. It's not the same, and everyone will call you punk-ass if you don't follow through.*]

WHIP IT UP

- Mix the crust ingredients together and spread in a greased 9 × 13 baking dish. Bake at 325 degrees for approximately 20 minutes. The crust will be light golden brown. Cool for 20 minutes.

- Mix the creamy layer ingredients and spread over the cooled crust.
- Mix the chocolate pudding according to the directions on the box.

   [PAUL'S NOTE: *Now, this is important, so pay attention. Do not make the chocolate pudding ahead of time because pudding only sets up once. If you make it ahead of time and try to transfer it, it will be runny, and you'll be eating your Chocolate Surprise through a straw. It sucks…literally.*]

- Pour the whipping cream into a chilled bowl and beat it with a mixer on high speed. Continue beating the whipping cream until peaks begin to form. Add the powdered sugar a little at a time and continue beating on low speed. Continue to add powdered sugar to taste. Spread over the chocolaty goodness layer. Fight over the bowl and the beaters.

Canna Cake

There is nothing easier than the Canna Cake. It's a can of this and a can of that, hence the name "canna." This is a recipe for you guys when you want to look like you're really participating in the pot-luck without really having to exert much effort (or for when your dumb ass misses the chance to sign up for plates/utensils or drinks. Mmnt!).

GET IT OUT

- 1 box yellow cake mix
- 15 oz. can cream of coconut
- 7 oz. can coconut (though bagged coconut is fine)

- 14 oz. can sweetened condensed milk
- 12 oz. whipped topping

WHIP IT UP

- Mix and bake the yellow cake mix according to the directions.
- While the cake is still hot, take the back end of a wooden spoon and poke holes throughout the cake from top to bottom.
- Mix the cream of coconut and condensed milk together and spread evenly over the top. After the cake sits for a few minutes, it will absorb these ingredients.
- After cooling, cover the cake with the whipped topping and top with coconut.

◆ ◆ ◆

Merry Christmas Cookies (aka Paul's Salty Cookies)

First, Paul is including this recipe to prove that these cookies are not salty! Second, it's a little misleading that they appear in this chapter because they don't really qualify as an "easy" potluck recipe. They're a royal pain in the butt because you have to make the dough, cool it, and then roll it out. Paul says they're called Merry Christmas Cookies because they're so difficult that you only want to make them once a year. They are, however, worth every second when you bite into the delicate sugar cookie with the brown butter icing, and they're perfect for taking to your next potluck.

[NICOLE'S NOTE: *There is nothing merry about this salty mess, so only take them to a potluck you don't want to be invited back to!*]

[PAUL'S NOTE: *Mmnt! They are* not *salty!! Try these cookies, and e-mail me your reaction. I'm sure you'll find that Nicole's hateful comments are just a guise for her obvious jealousy of my culinary talents.*]

[NICOLE'S NOTE: *They are so salty I had to go to the doctor for blood pressure medicine afterward. Double Mmnt!*]

[PAUL'S NOTE: *Whatever! People call me every year to ask me when I'm making them. If I had a store where these were the only thing I sold, I could have retired by now!*]

[NICOLE'S NOTE: *Very nice.*]

GET IT OUT

Cookie

- 1½ level cups sifted flour
- ½ cup butter
- ¾ cup sifted powdered sugar
- 1 egg yolk
- ½ tsp. salt
- 1 tsp. vanilla

Brown Butter Icing

- ¼ cup butter
- 2½ cups powdered sugar
- 1 tsp. vanilla
- 3–4 tbsp. milk or cream
- Sugar sprinkles (any color)

WHIP IT UP

Cookie

- Mix the cookie ingredients together into a putty-like consistency.
- Cool for 1 hour in the refrigerator to make the dough easier to work with.
- Roll the dough out and cut into 24 pieces.
- Bake at 350 degrees for 10 to 12 minutes until golden brown.
- Cool for 20 minutes.

Brown Butter Icing

- Brown the butter in a large saucepan. Once it's browned, remove from heat.
- Mix in the powdered sugar and vanilla.
- Slowly add in milk/cream 1 tbsp. at a time until icing-like consistency forms.
- Spread immediately on top of cooled cookies.
- Add sugar sprinkles as desired.

April Fool's Day Recipes

Bird Poop
Who wouldn't appreciate walking into their next potluck and seeing a nice steaming pile of bird poo next to the mashed potatoes and gravy? This concoction's realistic white and black turds would do any pigeon proud, and it certainly offers up a good fake-out for April Fool's.

GET IT OUT

- 5 cups of your favorite crunchy cereal (we like Peanut Butter Cap'n Crunch)
- 3 cups rice puff cereal
- 2 cups pretzels
- 1 bag white chocolate chips
- 2½ cups mini marshmallows

WHIP IT UP

- Mix all the dry ingredients in a large bowl.
- Melt the white chocolate in the microwave for about 1 minute.
- Pour the melted chocolate over the dry ingredients and spread on wax paper to cool.
- Once it's cool, break into bird poop–like chunks. Yummy!

Cat Barf

This dish is really only appetizing for those who don't have cats and have never cleaned up a warm hairball before. The lifelike clumping of this yellow, hairy-looking mess is alarmingly real, but if you can get past the looks of it, it is tasty as all get-out! Here kitty, kitty…

GET IT OUT

- 1 large spaghetti squash
- 8 oz. cottage cheese
- 16 oz. mozzarella (grated)
- 8 oz. parmesan (grated)
- 1 quart spaghetti sauce
- ½ green pepper, chopped

WHIP IT UP

- Lop of the ends and cut the squash in half.
- Place squash cut-sides-down in a microwave-safe baking dish.
- Microwave on high for about 12 minutes, or until you can easily pierce the squash with a fork.
- Let cool for about 15 minutes, or until squash is cool enough to handle.
- Fork out the insides into a giant casserole dish.
- Add cottage cheese, spaghetti sauce, peppers, and half of the mozzarella and Parmesan cheeses. Mix until it looks like cat barf.
- Top with the remaining cheeses.

BAKE IT, BITCH!

- Bake at 350 degrees for about 45 minutes.

Dog Food Dip

Easier on the eyes than Bird Poop and Cat Barf, this yummy dip pairs nicely with bread or chips. We've seen some people add ketchup or hot sauce to the top and call it bloody stool, but we prefer the less foul version served in a dog food bowl.

GET IT OUT

- 2 lbs. lean ground beef
- 1 onion, chopped
- 1 (10.75 oz.) can condensed cream of mushroom soup
- 1 lb. processed cheese spread, cubed

- 1 (12 oz.) jar sliced jalapeno peppers, drained
- 1 new dog food dish (clean)

WHIP IT UP

- Place lean ground beef and onion in a large, deep skillet over medium-high heat. Cook until the beef is brown and the onion is soft. Drain and turn the heat to medium-low.
- Add condensed cream of mushroom soup. Mix in processed cheese food cubes and desired amount of jalapeno peppers. Cook and stir until all ingredients are blended well, about 10 minutes.
- Transfer the mixture to a medium bowl. Cover and chill in the refrigerator 8 hours or overnight.

BAKE IT, BITCH!

- Reheat the mixture in a slow cooker, mixing in about 1 tablespoon of water to thin, if necessary, before serving.
- Mound the mixture into a clean dog food dish. Woof!

Halloween Recipes

Slimy Limey Fruit Punch

The first time we saw someone take a sip of this, we were slightly repulsed, but after succumbing to our friend's power of persuasion, we agreed this was quite an intoxicating punch (especially if you throw in a little vodka!). The red gel can stain, so be careful you don't end up with any semi-permanent scars on your body or clothes while you're making it.

GET IT OUT

- Powdered lemonade mixed to make 2 quarts
- 1 peeled and sliced orange
- 1 sliced lime (approximately 8 slices)
- 1 pint raspberries
- 2 tubes red decorating gel
- ¼ cup sugar
- 1 tsp. meringue powder
- 2 liters seltzer
- 10 drops green food coloring
- 4 drops yellow food coloring

WHIP IT UP

- Squeeze red gel down the insides of twelve small, clear glasses. Let dry for about 10 minutes.
- In an extra-large bowl, combine lemonade mix, sugar, and meringue powder. Slowly pour in the seltzer, whisking continually until combined.
- Stir in green and yellow food coloring.
- Add sliced fruit and berries for color.
- Pour punch into glasses and serve.

Bone-Chilling Brew

The bone-chilling parts of this drink are the frozen, floating hands that appear to be trapped under the surface of the water. Brew this as the party starts so the hands aren't half melted before everyone gets there. It's eerily good!

GET IT OUT

- 3 cups water
- 3 clear plastic gloves
- 3 rubber bands or twist ties
- 2 (64 oz.) bottles punch-flavored juice, chilled
- 1 (12 oz.) can frozen lemonade concentrate, slightly thawed
- 4 (12 oz.) cans lemon-lime soda, chilled

WHIP IT UP

For floating hands:

- Pour water into gloves, adding enough water to fill the gloves loosely but not so full that the fingers won't move.
- Fasten gloves with rubber bands or twist ties.
- Line baking sheet with paper towels.
- Place filled gloves on paper towels.
- Freeze for 3 hours or until firm.

For punch:

- Combine punch-flavored juice and lemonade concentrate in large punch bowl.
- Gradually stir in soda.
- Carefully cut gloves off hands with scissors.
- Float hands in punch.

◆ ◆ ◆

Glossary

Here you have it: a glossary of our fifty favorite phrases. Tear it out and hang it in your home or office so you, too, can begin introducing these witty and sometimes inappropriate phrases to your family and coworkers!

1. **Assaulted**—To be in a state of repugnance over a situation or someone's appearance.
2. **Beat the Seven Shades of Shit Out of You**—To inflict huge amounts of pain on someone.
3. **Bitch 'Bout to Get Cut**—A phrase said to someone when you are one step away from violence and giving someone a good ass whoopin'.
4. **Boinking off the Reservation**—To cheat on your spouse or significant other.
5. **Bow-Legged Cha-Cha**—Another name for sex.
6. **Butt Cleavage**—An exposed butt crack.
7. **Burro**—The hardest working person on a team; the one who never says no.
8. **Camel Toe**—The unsightly imprint of a woman's second pair of lips (her nether regions) when it shows through her pants. (And God forbid it's mammoth-sized; if that happens, we call it a "Moose Knuckle.")
9. **Creeper**—The person in the office who creeps around and makes inappropriate remarks or statements at inappropriate times.
10. **Cry of a Lonesome Turd**—A fart.
11. **Curse of a Thousand Doughnuts**—A magical curse that will befall you if you don't help someone when they call out "Mondo!" or perform the secret Mondo! nonverbal cue. It will be like gaining the weight from eating a thousand doughnuts without any of the enjoyment of eating them.

12. **Defecation Roster**—To be on someone's shit list.
13. **D-O-N-E**—When you've had enough, and you just can't take anymore.
14. **Don't Hate the Jiggly**—Something said to try to prevent someone from being jealous of your body.
15. **Eight Pounds, Six Ounces**—Your hallelujah shout-out when something wonderful happens or goes your way; usually followed by the name of a deity in baby form, such as Baby Jesus or Baby Allah.
16. **Esurient**—To be ravenously hungry.
17. **Etch-A-Sketch Moment**—When you see something or when someone tells you a story with a vivid mental image you would rather forget, and you wish you could erase the image by shaking your head, like erasing an Etch-A-Sketch. Frequently accompanied by shaking your head back and forth while you say it.
18. **EYB**—Embrace your bigness!
19. **Food Coma**—The exhaustion that ensues after eating a satisfying meal.
20. **Foreplay**—The person in a meeting who just goes on and on and won't get to the point.
21. **Gigaflops**—The very busty coworker who continues to wear shirts like her tits are still perky, when in fact they've actually fallen and flopped to the side like an old tire.
22. **Go Bitchcakes**—To react with excessive or irrational behavior to a situation.
23. **Gravity Check**—When someone falls or stumbles, usually due to lack of coordination on his or her part.
24. **Hater-Ade**—A fictitious drink you can accuse someone of drinking when everything coming out of his or her mouth is negative and/or bitchy.
25. **Having a Box Lunch at the Y**—When someone goes down on a woman.
26. **Heffa Juice**—Gravy (and lots of it, please!).

27. **Hooves High!**—A phrase used proudly to declare your love affair with food, usually accompanied by the Hooves High hand sign.
28. **Horizontal Refreshment**—Another phrase for having sex.
29. **Hot Flash**—A condition that occurs when one begins laughing so hard that sound ceases to emanate from one's mouth.
30. **Hump Island**—Your list of five actors or actresses that you and your significant other have agreed you can have your way with should the opportunity ever arise.
31. **IDTS**—I don't think so!
32. **Keep Digging, Watson**—Acerbic retort to "No shit, Sherlock!"
33. **Kinderwhore**—A young girl, often underage, who dresses in seductive schoolgirl fashion to generate interest from the opposite sex.
34. **Knock You in the Head and Tell God You Died**—A phrase used when you're mad at someone and want to convey your anger in a funny manner.
35. **LMAOPIMP**—Laughing my ass off peeing in my pants.
36. **LOL**—Laughing out loud (and if you didn't already know this one, you need to return this book for a full refund).
37. **Mental Midget**—Someone who hasn't heard of LOL before.
38. **Minion**—A servile dependent or underling who does your bidding upon command.
39. **Mmnt!**—An expression of displeasure; it's easy and simple to say, and it sounds better than "You stupid bitch," or "Damn, now I'm gonna have to work all night because your dumb ass just screwed up!"
40. **Mondo!**—A secret verbal or nonverbal cue you can give a close friend to help you quickly get out of an undesirable situation.
41. **Phisher**—The office gossips who present themselves as being factual and established when they are really presenting you a virtual reality and fishing for anything to make their story more enticing for someone to bite…hook, line, and sinker.

42. **Really?**—Used any time you know the line or story someone is giving you is a hot mess, or any time you find yourself in a situation you can't believe is really happening.
43. **Resource Hog**—Office slut.
44. **ROFLWMM**—Rolling on the floor laughing wiping my mascara.
45. **Shaking**—The next-to-last step of the peeing process (for males). When you're done peeing, you have to shake your pistol a little to ensure you don't drip once you reholster it. The final step is rebuckling your pants and/or zipping your fly.
46. **Sonofabitch**—A one-word phrase used to describe someone who has done you wrong.
47. **SSR**—If the shit flows downhill and stops with you, then you, our friend, are the Sanitation Service Rep!
48. **To' Up from the Flo' Up**—Code for "tore up from the floor up," or put another way, "fucked up."
49. **Whore**—Someone who loves something greatly or who gives him or herself over to something freely.
50. **Wide-On**—The female equivalent of a man's hard-on.

About the Authors

 Since 2006, Paul Mitchell and Nicole White have been teaching fellow Hoofers how to build strong relationships with people, both inside and outside their team, through their unique brand of humor and the universal language of food. Most of all, they show people how they live out loud and how they're okay making fun of themselves. They share their tips and tricks for making it through the work day one hoof at a time.

They both have been published in the book *The ITIL Experience*, where they chronicled their formulas for success in their everyday jobs, building and implementing processes for different IT companies in the southeast. They both hold several certifications, including Global Project Management, Managing for Performance, Social Styles and Networking, 7 Habits of Highly Effective People, and Train the Trainer.

Paul and his wife, Marilyn, live with their three children and three dogs in Atlanta, Georgia. They also have two nieces and another nephew who think they live there, too. A chronic organizer, Paul is always looking for new projects to undertake. His favorite foods are Tortica de Moron cookies (Cuban sugar cookies) and ketchup (which he strongly believes should be its own food group).

Nicole lives with her three children in Atlanta, Georgia. She's an active member in a fraternal organization and loves Twilight and Ricky Bobby. She's dubbed her house "Cougar's Cave." (Team Edward and Team Jacob, baby!) Her favorite foods are macaroni and cheese and Chunky Monkey ice cream.

Connect with Paul and Nicole on their Hooves High Facebook site!